Our family has had the honor and privilege of knowing Nancy Alcorn for over 15 years. It is our belief that there is nothing closer to the heart of God than to help heal the brokenhearted. This is the driving force behind the work of Mercy Ministries, and we are proud to be connected with this life-changing organization.

Joel and Victoria Osteen
Senior Pastors, Lakewood Church
Houston, TX

With the dysfunction of families, children having babies, rampant sexual abuse, and the lack of morality, it is difficult to see any hope for young women to have self-esteem and grow in wholeness. Mercy Ministries is not afraid to deal with the ugly, tough stuff–sexual abuse, cutting, starvation. Nancy and her Mercy Ministries team get to the core issues. If you have a daughter, work with girls, or are a young woman struggling with these issues ... you want to hear what Nancy has to say. It is sure to change your life.

CeCe Winans
Grammy Award Winning Artist
Nashville, TN

As a father of two young women, I certainly know what girls face today. So many do not receive the right kind of love from their families and make bad choices without realizing it. The guilt and shame from these devastating choices often lead to serious struggles with self-destructive behaviors. I have watched Nancy Alcorn and Mercy Ministries bring hope and healing to struggling young women for many years–young women who were completely without hope. Mercy Ministries offers great inspiration, hope, and a way to true healing for all who want to be free.

Dave Ramsey
Financial Expert and
Best-Selling Author
Nashville, TN

It's really hard to express what we feel in our hearts about Mercy Ministries. It's a place filled with peace, warmth, and unconditional love. We're excited to see what God is doing through this incredible organization, and we're honored to share about it whenever we can. Lives are truly changed through Mercy Ministries!

Point of Grace
Contemporary Christian
Recording Artists
Nashville, TN

When I was 17 years old on the night before starting my senior year of high school, I got pregnant the first time I had sex. I was already distraught, as my parents had taken my younger brother, who was dying from Hodgkin's disease, to seek treatment. Our family was falling apart, I couldn't drive a car, had never had a job, and got $1.50 weekly allowance.

I am so glad today that I chose life against all odds. That baby grew up to be Wynonna Judd.

Knowing that an unplanned pregnancy can be one of the most difficult decisions a woman can face, I support Mercy Ministries of America.

Naomi Judd
Country Music Recording Artist
Franklin, TN

Echoes of Mercy is a testimony to the faithfulness of God. It will inspire you to make a difference in the world. Nancy Alcorn is an awesome woman of God who believes in the potential of every human being. She has committed her life to the service and transformation of broken young women, helping them discover their true value in Christ. *Echoes of Mercy* demonstrates how a living Jesus heals a dying world.

Christine Caine
Director Equip &
Empower Ministries
Sydney, Australia

In a day when most people simply point out problems of this life, Nancy Alcorn is dedicated to offering solutions to seemingly hopeless situations. Founder and President of Mercy Ministries of America, Nancy is a woman with a mandate from the Holy Spirit to salvage the lives of the unborn, while bringing the hope of the Gospel of Jesus Christ to young women. Her book *Echoes of Mercy* is sure to bless and inspire everyone who reads it.

Jesus said, "Permit the children to come unto me for such is the kingdom of God." God is interested in children, that's why He created us.

Nancy, I would say keep doing what you are doing. At all costs whatever it takes. For when you touch a child, you touch the heart of God.

Jesse Duplantis
Evangelist
New Orleans, Louisiana

ECHOES OF MERCY

ECHOES OF
MERCY

BY NANCY ALCORN

Mercy Ministries
Lives transformed. Hope restored.

Printed in the United States of America.

Library of Congress Cataloging-in-Publication Data
Alcorn, Nancy.
    Echoes of Mercy / by Nancy Alcorn. — 1st ed.
      p.   cm.

    1. Mercy Ministries. 2. Church work with delinquent girls—Louisiana—Monroe. 3. Alcorn, Nancy.   I. Title.
BV4464.5.A43 1992
259/.23-dc20   92-31884
                                               CIP

10 9 8 7 6 5 4 3

Dedication

This book is dedicated to all those young girls out there who are hurting and desperate and still looking for an answer. *There is hope for you. There is an answer.* My prayer is that at least some of you will find your answer while reading the pages of this book.

Table of Contents

Acknowledgments

All honor and praise to Jesus, who is the life changer.

To my heroes: All the "Mercy Girls" who found the courage to willingly come and face very painful issues in their lives, allowing God to give them not just hope, but a future. (Jeremiah 29:11)

To our supporters: For your financial gifts and your prayers. Without our partners, the work of Mercy Ministries would not be possible.

To my staff: For all of your hard work, dedication, and daily sacrifices.

Foreword by
Cal Thomas

America is confronted with so many problems—economic, political, moral, and social—and they seem to be growing at such an alarming rate that the average person feels powerless to deal with them. Most of us look only for protection from the creeping monsters that seek to consume us. Too many of us retreat from the cities into the suburbs to avoid crime and into apathy and coldness of heart toward those who most need our help. We pretend that if we can only put such problems out of sight, or at least no closer than the television set or newspaper, we can put our obligation to address them out of our minds.

However, the command of Jesus Christ is to act as a preservative in the culture. The purpose of a preservative is to slow down the process of spoilage which eventually leads to rotten meat. Those of us who read and believe the Bible know that the Earth in its present condition is spoiling and will eventually rot. It would ultimately be destroyed were it not for the intervention of Jesus Christ who gives to it (and us) a new, transformed, and unending life, free of physical death, pollution of the environment, and moral decay.

In the meantime, each of us who are children of God through our acceptance of Jesus Christ and repentance of our sins is commissioned to act as a preserving agent. It is a commission and a command. It is *not* an option.

Why are we to do this? It is so that the Gospel might have freer rein to be shared to the uttermost parts of the Earth, because God is not willing that any should perish, but that all might come to Him through His Son.

As a journalist for more than three decades, I am convinced that the moral, social, and political problems that confront this nation are the result of individual believers who have lost their "saltiness." Too many are like that sodium-free stuff people use who must avoid real salt for health reasons. It looks like salt, it tastes like salt, but all of its preserving qualities have been removed. A recent Gallup Poll found that only ten percent of Christians have what Gallup called "transforming faith."

Nancy Alcorn is among that ten percent. Her enthusiasm for Christ is that of a young girl who has fallen in love for the first time. Her compassion for those who are lost and for those girls and women who are saved, but have strayed, is as deep and real as anyone I know.

Mercy Ministries is aptly named. It extends the love and mercy—not judgment—of Jesus Christ to every person it touches. It is doing the work of God, not only in Nashville, but by example and reputation to others who have heard of it and have met Nancy and some of the women who have entered its doors, women who have left with a new purpose for living and a changed life.

At the end of our lives, it will not matter at all how much money we made, how many famous and powerful people we met (or whether we became famous and powerful ourselves). It will matter a great deal what we did with the knowledge and power and grace and, yes, mercy God has extended to us.

A little verse I learned in Sunday school years ago said, "Only one life, 'twill soon be past; only what's done for Christ will last."

Nancy Alcorn and Mercy Ministries of America are doing the work of Christ which will multiply and last beyond Nancy's own life. This book is the story of Mercy Ministries, but it is more than that. It is also the story of what one person can do who is sold out to God. My hope is that it will serve as a testimony to others who need to be about the business of Christ and be done with lesser things.

Cal Thomas
Washington, D.C.

Foreword by Gloria Gaither

When I was asked to write the foreword to this book, I could not help but think how appropriate God's timing is in light of the fact that Bill and I are presently awaiting the birth of our first child's first child.

At a special time in our own family, it is not difficult at all for me to write about how precious life is—all life, regardless of the circumstances surrounding the conception of that life. The best way I know to describe the amazing impact of a newborn baby on so many people is to share with you a portion of my own personal diary written to my first grandbaby as I eagerly await its arrival . . .

> "A place to be" is very important to us all. You will take for granted (as all children should be able to do) that you have a place to belong. You will have a place in this house. You will have a place at this table, and every morning it will be empty until you bound down the stairs and slip into your chair for breakfast. You will have a place to be in the car. At first it will be a special car seat for infants, then a bigger one for toddlers— a seat made to government specifications to protect you.

You will have a place in the circle of your family. Even now there is a change taking place in the relationship of your parents to each other. They are holding tightly to each other while at the same time hollowing out a safe place in the circle of their love for you. As you gradually slip into that place—that process has already begun—that circle will widen, yet grow deeper and stronger. It will be your coming that will teach them that giving love away only makes it multiply and expand.

There will be a place for you in the extended family. Your Grandma Jennings is already putting away little things for you, planning where you will sleep when you come to visit and thinking about how she can make more trips to Indiana. She is a Tupperware District Manager, and has no doubt noticed more and more things in her Tupperware catalogs that "might come in handy" when you get here. And your place at our house is ready and waiting for you. There are sheets and a soft comforter on your cradle, your high chair sits near the kitchen table, and I've been thinking of ordering a baby seat for the swing set that has been empty all too long.

Your great-grandparents have a place for you, too. How I hope you will know them! I want you to remember watching the ducks and geese, birds and squirrels out of your Great-grandmother Sickal's big window and hear her tell you stories of the wondrous ways of God's creatures. I want you to remember the warmth of Grandma and Grandpa Gaither's farmhouse, smell the meatloaf and green beans on the stove, and watch Grandma's hands cutting egg noodles and beating the batter for German chocolate cake. I hope you will get to go with Grandpa to feed the calves or horses, pick fresh tomatoes from the garden, or ride the mower around the pine trees in the yard. There are also special spaces for you at Uncle Dave's and Aunt Evelyn's house, at Uncle Danny and Vonnie's, and in the circle of Tim and Dianne's and Don and Lorie's families.

There will be a place to belong in the arms of the Family of God, and this is the most important of all places to belong, because this circle embraces all the other family circles and outlasts them all. Your mother is already planning the day when, with your daddy, you will be brought to the altar to be dedicated to the Lord. On that day and in the company of a body of believers, they will make public the commitment they have already made to God to "bring you up in the nurture and the admonition of the Lord." And that body of believers will make a public statement of their commitment and responsibility to teach, encourage, protect, and lead you in the "paths of righteousness for His Name's sake."

Finally, you have a place to belong in the very heart of God, for He planned for your being "from before the foundations of the earth" and has watched you as you are even now being formed in your mother's womb. You are precious to Him and have been marked and singled out for a purpose unique to you alone. At great price God has made provision for you to be the companion of His heart and He has plans to walk and talk with you, to "commune with you in the cool of the day." And no matter what voices call for your attention, no matter what forces conspire to distract you, you will always be restless, you will never be content until you settle into the most important of all places to belong—the center of the very heart of God.

Life is precious, much too precious to throw away. In this world in which we live, I am grateful that God has raised up Mercy Ministries of America to provide homes for young girls in trouble, places where countless numbers of babies will have the opportunity to experience what our new grandchild will experience—a loving family.

For those who read this book, *Echoes of Mercy* will stir you and challenge you. God can take less than ideal situations and turn them into powerful testimonies for His glory. Your heart will be warmed by the girls who chose unselfishly through much prayer to bless a childless couple with the greatest gift anyone could ever give—the gift of life. For those girls who chose to keep their babies, God has promised to be a father to the fatherless, a husband to the husbandless. He will make up whatever is lacking through the greatest family of all — the family of God.

Gloria Gaither
Alexandria, Indiana

Introduction

Catching the Vision

Also I heard the voice of the Lord, saying: "Whom shall I send, and who will go for Us?" Then I said, "Here am I! Send me." (Isaiah 6:8)

This book contains a vision for the church of Jesus Christ. It is a vision of mercy. It is a vision of ministering to broken lives that have been devastated by sin. It is a vision of being used by the Holy Spirit to reach out and bring forgiveness and restoration to those broken lives. More to the point, it is a vision of actively working to tangibly demonstrate the overwhelming mercy of God in both word and deed. It is also a vision of the church transforming people through the power of the Gospel of Jesus Christ.

The message is simple: every Christian is obligated to extend God's mercy to those who need to experience the forgiving love of Jesus Christ and the transforming work of the Holy Spirit in their lives. Just as we have been shown mercy by God, so must we show mercy to others. Jesus said "Blessed are the merciful: for they shall obtain mercy" (Matt. 5:7 KJV). And just as Christ came to us and acted on our behalf, so must we go to those in need and actively intervene on their behalf.

Since I began working with troubled youth in 1973, many interesting observations have afforded me insight into the reasons social problems exist. God didn't intend for us to abuse our bodies with drugs, alcohol, illicit sex, and extra pounds. Yet these abuses are increasing, resulting in complex problems.

These problems are much deeper than what lies on the surface. They represent not only *what* people are doing but *why* they are doing it. There are root causes in people that bring about the multiple social problems our society is facing today. We must deal with the root causes and not just their symptoms. Drug abuse and teen pregnancy are only outward manifestations of greater inward problems. The inward problems may be things like self-hate, fear, insecurity, guilt, unforgiveness, and hurts from the past.

Many women have been victims of incest, rape, physical and sexual child abuse, and other tragic experiences in unpleasant childhoods; they have been deeply wounded. In order for these women to have happy lives, they must deal with the past hurts, be relieved of the guilt, and destroy the root causes. This can only happen through a personal experience of the love and forgiveness of God—then they can move toward success in other areas.

As you read of God's unfailing faithfulness to Mercy Ministries and the rich rewards that come from being faithful to Him, I hope and pray that the Holy Spirit will give you a vision of healing the brokenhearted, proclaiming deliverance to the captives, and setting at liberty those who are bound (see Isa. 61:1). The purpose of this book is not to promote any one ministry, but to provoke you to ask yourself how you can take part in Christ's command to show mercy and bring restoration to broken lives.

1

The Calling
God's Hand on My Life

Then the word of the Lord came to me, saying: "Before I formed you in the womb I knew you; before you were born I sanctified you; and I ordained you a prophet to the nations." (Jeremiah 1:4-5)

The contrast between the summer sunset and my grim surroundings was stark. A dull metal chain-link fence topped with coiled barbed wire enclosed the many gray buildings of the huge correctional facility: five dormitories, a large separate school facility, a guardhouse, a cafeteria, and many other buildings. The state government's attempt to make the correctional facility look pleasant through nice landscaping could not mask the locked gates, the patrolling guards, and the institutional atmosphere of a place that incarcerated nearly three hundred girls from all over Tennessee—it seemed bleak and hopeless.

With one last longing glance at the sunset, I walked into the gym, thinking about my work. I was one of fifty-five staff workers trying to help girls who had been sent to that facility by the juvenile courts. I loved the girls and wanted desperately to help them, but I often doubted that my work was making a difference in their lives.

As I reached my office, the phone interrupted my thoughts.

Within moments, I was rushing across the compound toward one of the several dormitories. Nothing I had yet experienced as the athletic director of a correctional facility for juvenile delinquent girls had prepared me for the chaos that I was witnessing.

About a dozen teenage girls were yelling in panic-stricken voices, "Get them off me! Get them away from me!" They were screaming, writhing, and clawing themselves and anyone who came near. I could not see what the girls were wailing about, and in their state it was useless to try to talk to them. They seemed to be suffering horrible hallucinations— seeing huge snakes and spiders slithering and crawling all over them. Every staff member available was trying to restrain the girls to keep them from injuring themselves in their hysteria. I joined the commotion, holding down a girl, restraining her from clawing her face.

We learned from others in the dormitory that the girls had discovered a common plant, known as "locoweed," growing around the campus laundromat. One of the girls had learned that it would give them a high if they swallowed enough of its seeds. Some of the girls wanted to get high so badly they were willing to try anything. For weeks they had been harvesting these seeds, hoping to gather enough to get them stoned. Their experiment did not turn out as they had hoped it would.

Once enough staff members were present to control the hallucinating girls, we hurriedly put them in state vehicles and drove to the local hospital in Tullahoma, Tennessee. These hysterical young women desperately trying to pull slithering snakes from their bodies must have felt utterly hopeless to risk permanently harming themselves in exchange for a temporary high.

I waited at the hospital with several other staff workers as the girls were admitted to the emergency room. The doctor discovered that the weed they had ingested was not only hallucinogenic but poisonous. Their stomachs were pumped and they were sent by ambulance to a larger hospital in Nashville where they could be better examined for any residual effects of the toxin.

I followed the ambulance in my car, wondering how this reform school could possibly claim to be reforming these girls. Despite my doubts, however, I knew God had opened doors for me to work there. As the white lines of the highway appeared in my headlights and disappeared into the darkness behind me, I reminded myself of His hand on my life.

Life Without Mercy

I was born and raised in a good church-going home in Tennessee. Anyone looking only at outward appearances would have believed I was a committed Christian. In high school I continued to attend church regularly with my family. If asked, "Is Nancy a good Christian girl?" any of the adult members of my church would have replied, "Oh yes; of course she is— she's even president of the youth group." Being president of my church's youth fellowship didn't mean a thing. I had not given my heart to Jesus—I was too busy living my life my own way. I did not understand who Jesus Christ was, what He had done for me, and what He would do for me if I would only ask Him.

As a result of going my own way, I felt increasingly empty and aimless. At first I didn't realize my life lacked purpose. I was popular in school, I always had friends among the "in" crowd, and I was repeatedly elected to hold office in student government. From outward appearances there was nothing wrong with my life.

Performance in athletic activities gave me value, and my self-esteem depended on my success in sports. From a relatively young age, sports were the center of my identity, and I planned my future around a career in athletics. I was continually involved in various athletic competitions at my school. I started for the ninth grade basketball team even though I was only in seventh grade. I already knew what I wanted to do with my life:

"I'm going to play college basketball while majoring in physical education. Afterward, I'll become a coach or an athletic director." I took comfort in knowing where I was headed.

In ninth grade my world was shattered. I seriously injured my knee and every time it started to heal I injured it again. I loved basketball so much I couldn't wait for my knee to heal properly before I got back on the court. I went to an orthopedic specialist at St. Thomas Hospital, who also happened to be a team physician for the Vanderbilt University Athletic Department. Since I was an avid Vanderbilt fan, I really thought that was a big deal because he was the best. Dr. Lipscomb prescribed a weight-lifting regimen to rehabilitate my knee.

I continued injuring my knee. Several times I ended up in Dr. Lipscomb's office after ill-fated attempts to play basketball. My knee would be tightly swollen and blue and he would withdraw several syringes full of bloody fluid that had collected at the joint. Though I hated the pain I suffered and the horrible sight of what I was doing to my knee, I kept trying to play sports. My determination led to two major knee surgeries. Finally Dr. Lipscomb sat me down in his office and told me what I didn't want to hear: "Nancy, due to the obvious weakness of your knee and the repeated injuries, it is clear that you can't go on like this. You need to stop participating in sports."

"Surely, this can't be true," I thought. "There's got to be something that can be done to fix my knee." Sports were the one thing I knew I was good at and basketball was my life. It was unimaginable to me that I could no longer play. As I realized I would never again be able to play basketball, I grew hopeless and bitter.

Once I faced the fact that I could no longer play, in order to have something to do with the game I loved, I became the manager of the girls' basketball team. I went through intense emotional struggles before I could consent to merely carrying water bottles and distributing towels to the players. I hated being reduced to having such an unimportant and invisible position on the team. I was used to being at the center of attention on the court, not being stuck on the sidelines. It took everything in me to remain involved in the game only as a supporter, and I was envious of the girls who were out on the court. Many times as I watched the team play, I wondered why I subjected myself to such agony. But I couldn't stand the thought of not being connected to the team in some way, so I stuck it out as water girl.

Though I could still pursue a career in athletics as a coach or a trainer, my immediate future seemed bleak because the possibility of playing college basketball had been snatched from me. I no longer had a driving goal to give my life meaning. Many of my girlfriends were hoping to find husbands and get married soon after high school. While I was not opposed to being a wife and mother, I did not feel I should marry young. There was something else I was supposed to accomplish, but I had no idea what it might be. I became increasingly angry at the world since I had lost the ability to do the thing I really loved to do.

In response to the anger I felt, I rebelled. My rebellion was probably similar to that of most teenagers of that time. Once in a while I went out smoking and drinking. I knew it was wrong, but at the time I didn't care. Since I would be unable to pursue my ambition of a life in sports, I no longer cared about staying in shape. Though I periodically dabbled in alcohol and tobacco, I never got mixed up in either heavily enough to become addicted.

By the summer I graduated from high school, I had long recognized the emptiness of the teenage drinking parties I occasionally attended. Not only were they unfulfilling, they were not exciting enough to overcome the oppressive lack of direction in my life. Furthermore, I knew what I was doing was not only wrong but against the standards I had set for myself throughout my teenage years. I had always been a leader, but by drinking and smoking I was conforming to other people's standards and behaving more like a follower.

The one positive thing I had going for me during my high school years was that I had a job with the Cracker Barrel restaurant in my hometown of Manchester, Tennessee. Though I didn't think about it much at the time, this was good experience in preparing me for future responsibility, and it also enabled me to save enough money to buy my first car and pay my own way through college.

Some of my friends were experimenting with drugs, and I considered joining them once I got to college. But another part of me really wanted my life to have lasting significance and value. My feelings were mixed.

Though I didn't realize it at the time, sports was the idol which I had used in the place of God to give my life meaning and direction. Through the knee injury, that idol was taken from me, leaving nothing to disguise my emptiness. I was miserable and frustrated.

The Turning Point

While I was trying to cope with my aimlessness, other forces were working to give my life a direction different from anything I had imagined. I had a Christian friend who, though I was not aware of it at the time, had been praying for my conversion for three years. Cleta was a high school cheerleader who had been looking for an opportunity to witness to me.

Three weeks before I was to leave for college, she called me: "Nancy, there's going to be a week-long lay-witness meeting at the church. It should be pretty interesting. Why don't you come with me?"

I hesitated to answer. Cleta was always inviting me to church events and I was never eager to attend them. "Maybe I'll see you there," I said unenthusiastically. I did not want to go, but didn't want to turn Cleta down either.

Cleta knew what I was thinking and took steps to persuade me to go with her. That night when my mother came home from her fabric business, she told me, "Cleta dropped by the

shop today and mentioned that she's invited you to go to the
lay-witness meeting at the church. I think you should go."

At first I was angry that Cleta had used my mother to try
to compel me to accept her invitation. But I decided that it
couldn't hurt to attend the meetings. For once, her persistence
in prayer, persuasion, and pressure paid off. I reluctantly
agreed to go.

For the first time in my life, I saw *lay people* standing up
in front of the church sharing their testimonies—bearing witness to what Jesus Christ had done in their lives. Until then
the only people I had seen talk about God in church were professional preachers. I had always figured they preached
because it was their job. Why would anyone stand up and talk
about God in front of a crowd unless he was getting paid for
it? Yet here were people of all different ages and backgrounds, speaking about how they had a personal, day-to-day
relationship with Jesus Christ and how they had experienced
His forgiveness and transforming power.

I was particularly moved by the messages of many of the
young people who explained how they had been set free from
sin, guilt, and fear and how Jesus Christ filled the void in
their lives—giving them purpose and direction. One young
woman especially touched my heart. She said she had under-
gone an abortion. The father of her child was a married man
who had promised to divorce his wife and marry her. When
she told him she was pregnant, he told her he couldn't care
less what happened to her. Abandoned and alone with her
future suddenly gone, she had an abortion, thinking it would
help. Though the abortion got rid of the child, it added more
heartache to the guilt, shame, and empty isolation she
already felt. Eventually, a failed suicide attempt landed her in
the hospital.

When she was in the depths of despair, a lady came to visit
her in the hospital. She told her, "I don't care what you've
done. I don't care who you've been with. There's no sin that

is so black and so dark that Jesus Christ will not forgive you and cleanse you. He'll take your life and He will give you a reason to live."

I was cut to the heart by the words that had led to her conversion. Now what would I do? There I was—all set to go to college—and now the Holy Spirit was convicting me that I needed to repent, release my life to Christ, and rely on Him in a day-to-day relationship.

I left the church service that night struggling. The Holy Spirit was working on me, but I wasn't sure I wanted to make such a commitment. I was headed nowhere and my life needed to be turned around, but I wasn't sure I was willing to give up my independence. If I do something, I want to do it all the way; I wanted to avoid a shallow "conversion." Unless I was absolutely sure I was ready to carry through with the commitment involved in accepting Christ, I didn't want to do it. I spent the next three days unable to either eat or sleep, under the strong conviction that I needed to ask God for a new life and for forgiveness of my sins. In the middle of the week I decided to stop fighting against what I knew I needed to do.

I suppose most people who decide to surrender their lives to Jesus Christ pray where they are. But I called Cleta and asked her and another girl in the group, Button, to take me to the church. Though she probably wondered why I wanted to go to church in the middle of the afternoon, she took me. In my religious mind-set, I thought I had to be inside a church building in order to become a Christian.

Once at the church, I walked inside with Cleta and Button and immediately went to the altar and started to pray. It was late August, the church had no air conditioner, and it was easily a hundred degrees. I must have been crying, praying, confessing my sins, begging for forgiveness, and asking Jesus to take control of my life for at least fifteen minutes when Button tapped me on the shoulder and said, "You know what? He heard you the first moment you asked Him, and He forgave you. You don't need to beg Him; you just need to receive it."

I looked at Button and said, "But I don't feel any different. Aren't you supposed to feel all warm inside or something?"

"Some people have experiences like that, but it's not a *feeling* that causes you to know something happened—it's what the Word says." She picked up her Bible and asked me, "Do you believe this is God's Word?"

"Yes."

"Do you believe God would lie?"

"No."

"Then let me show you something." Button opened her Bible. "Here in 1 John 1:9, 'If you confess your sins to God, He is faithful and just to forgive you and to cleanse you from all unrighteousness.' You just confessed your sin. You did your part and He did His part—He forgave you and cleansed you. So whether you feel anything or not, it's still true."

As Button read the Bible to me, a light came on inside me and I realized that what she had just read to me was true—God had forgiven me. I was now a "real" Christian. Thus I was born again that Wednesday afternoon in the heat of the day—August 9, 1972.

Going Public

After I prayed to receive Christ and His forgiveness, one of the first things I told Cleta and Button was, "I respect you guys for praying out loud and I respect you for telling your stories, but don't ever ask me to pray out loud, don't ever ask me to speak in front of a group, and don't *ever* ask me to give my testimony because this is going to be a private thing with me." To me it was unthinkable that I could stand up in public and talk about God.

Button laughed when I said my faith was going to stay private and said, "Nancy, God has already shown me that one day you're going to be like Paul." My knowledge of the

Bible was so shallow that I didn't even know who Paul was, and I told her so.

Button laughed again. "Never mind, we'll get you a Bible that is easy to understand." She seemed amused at my lack of knowledge.

The next day she took me to a Christian bookstore and bought me a Living Bible, the kind with the green cover. I'll never forget that day as long as I live. I spent the next three weeks until I went to college devouring that Bible. For the first time in my life, I could not put it down—reading it both day and night.

Discovering the Bible was a strange and wonderful experience. I had never known God's Word would speak directly to me and give me answers for my personal life. I was like a kid with a new toy! It was exciting!

After becoming a Christian, I worried about going to college. I knew that by praying to receive Christ I had undertaken a responsibility to live differently than I had before. I was used to being accepted by the popular crowd at school and was unsure if I could take a stand for Christ and keep my old friends. Although I no longer desired to go out and party, I wondered if I might be tempted to go back to that life-style.

When I was thinking those thoughts, I opened my Bible, and my eyes were drawn to the following verses:

> You won't be spending the rest of your life chasing after evil desires, but will be anxious to do the will of God. You have had enough in the past of the evil things the godless enjoy—sex, sin, lust, getting drunk, wild parties, drinking bouts, and the worship of idols, and other terrible sins. Of course, your former friends will be very surprised when you don't eagerly join them any more in the wicked things they do, and they will laugh at you in contempt and scorn. But just remember that they must face the Judge of all, living and dead; they will be punished for the way they have lived. (1 Peter 4:2-5 TLB)

I was shocked. I could not believe Scripture actually talked about drinking and partying. I had thought the Bible was just about history. It was incredible to discover that, whatever issues concerned me or whatever questions I had, I could find answers by reading that book. God spoke to me from the pages of the Bible, assuring me I wouldn't fall into my old life and telling me not to worry about what my non-Christian friends might think of my new life.

A week before leaving for Middle Tennessee State University I had an opportunity to go to a Sunday night service in another church that many of the same people who had spoken at the lay-witness meeting would be attending. I agreed to go, making clear to my friends that I did not want to get up in front of the congregation to share my testimony. Two weeks of growing in Christ had not changed my feelings about talking in front of groups.

God had other plans that night. Somehow the man in charge of the service had heard about my recent conversion but not about my reluctance to engage in public speaking.

"We had a really exciting thing happen a couple weeks ago and the person involved is here tonight. I'd like for her to come up here and share with you all what has happened to her." I had no idea the service leader was referring to me. When he called my name, I was shocked, but what could I do? I didn't have much of a choice. Slowly, I stood up and walked to the front of the church. As he put the microphone in my hand, the lay leader told me, "I want you to share from your heart what God did for you two weeks ago."

I stood there in front of the church, looking over the congregation, wondering what I should say. It was too late to back out. I was angry and afraid—angry that I had been called to speak against my will and afraid to give my testimony in front of so many people. Then something happened inside me. Suddenly, sharing my testimony in front of a group of people did not seem like such an impossible task. After all, I thought,

they all love me so I don't need to worry about being rejected or laughed at. And I needed to tell people about what God
had done in my life. I talked about how I had been born again.
Although I had walked to the front of the church not knowing
what to say, my testimony lasted at least twenty minutes.
Some people in the congregation were so touched they were
wiping away tears.

By the time I finished I was no longer angry that I had been
called to speak in front of the church. Looking back, I am sure
the Lord was at work that night, adjusting me to the idea of
publicly sharing my testimony. The leader who asked me to
tell my story could not have done me a greater favor. If I had
not been pushed over the edge that night I don't know when I
might have overcome my reluctance to speak before groups.
I had no idea I would eventually speak before thousands at
churches and even on national television. Finding the courage
to share my testimony was an important lesson.

Despite the experience I have gained teaching and speaking to groups of various sizes since that night and all the positive feedback I have received from those who have listened
to me, I have never thought of myself as a polished speaker.
Rather, I am an example of how the Holy Spirit can use "the
foolish things of the world to put to shame the wise," and "the
weak things of the world to put to shame the things which are
mighty" (1 Cor. 1:27).

In addition to helping me when I eventually became
involved in full-time ministry, learning to publicly share my
faith in the Lord Jesus Christ became an immediate benefit
for me when I went to college a week later.

College Life

I still had much to learn about the Christian life. Though I
had shared my testimony in church, I still dreaded the thought
of telling others outside church that I was a Christian. This fear
was especially acute in relation to my new college roommate.

Six months earlier I had filled out a form specifying my roommate preference for my first year in college: I wanted to room with someone I didn't know and who wasn't from my hometown. I was sick of the small town mentality and I wanted to broaden my horizons.

The university responded with a letter saying that I would be rooming with a girl named Debbie Peterson from Nashville. I was glad I didn't know her, but really didn't give the matter much thought at the time. Debbie, however, was spending a lot of time thinking about her roommate assignment. Debbie received a similar letter, telling her that Nancy Alcorn from Manchester, Tennessee, would be her roommate. Her mother, who had divorced years earlier, had raised Debbie in a Christian home and was concerned that Debbie might be assigned a roommate who wanted to drink and party. She tried to talk her into living at home and commuting, but Debbie held her ground.

"Mom, if you really believe what you have always taught me about God, then we need to quit worrying and trust Him. We have this girl's name, so let's pray for her. God will take care of it!"

The two of them prayed for and about "Nancy Alcorn from Manchester" all summer.

Several months later I met Debbie during freshman orientation, the day we both moved into the dorm. We did not get much chance to talk beyond simply saying "Hello." I knew I needed to tell her I was a Christian, but I was terrified of how she might respond. I was used to being liked, and I was afraid she would think I was a religious nut. I was so nervous that for several days I stayed out until 1:00 or 2:00 A.M., when I was sure Debbie would be asleep so I wouldn't have to talk to her. I pretended to be asleep until she left the room in the morning.

Finally, after Debbie left the room one morning, I got out the Living Bible Button had given me. I still didn't know how to tell Debbie I was a Christian. Flipping through my Bible, my eyes fell on a passage in Matthew: "If anyone publicly acknowledges me as his friend, I will openly acknowledge him as my friend before my Father in heaven. But if anyone publicly denies me, I will openly deny him before my Father in heaven" (Matt. 10:32-33 TLB). I realized that regardless of how scared I was, I had to tell Debbie I was a Christian. I could not be ashamed of my commitment to live for Christ— these verses told me as much!

"All right," I told God, "I'll stop dodging this girl. But you have to show me how I'm supposed to tell her I'm a Christian because I don't know how."

After talking to God, I remembered a card someone had given me that said, "If you were arrested for being a Christian, would there be enough evidence to convict you?" I suddenly had an idea.

I taped the card to the outside of the door of our dorm room near the keyhole where she couldn't miss seeing it as she came in. Then I sat on my bed and waited for her return. I imagined her storming into the room after reading the card and telling me I was a weird fanatic. Nevertheless, I sat on my bed and waited. Once she saw the card, at least I could get this ordeal over with. I would not dodge the issue anymore. She would know where I stood.

I waited for probably about an hour—it seemed like forever—before Debbie finally came to the room. When I heard the key turning in the lock, my heart started beating fast. She walked over to the bed. I looked up at her, speechless, so scared that I was literally shaking.

"Did you put that card on the door?" she asked.

I swallowed hard and said, "Yes."

"Are you a Christian?"

"Ye-Yes"

"Praise the Lord!" Debbie yelled. She ran to the phone and dialed as fast as she could. "Mama! Mama, she's a Christian!" she exclaimed into the receiver. She listened for a moment, then said, "I don't know. I haven't asked her yet. I'll call and tell you later. Bye."

She hung up the phone and came back over to me. "I'm so excited! How long have you been a Christian?"

I smiled, overjoyed that instead of being rejected I was being received by a fellow Christian. "Three weeks," I said.

Debbie started crying. I was horrified. "What's the matter?" I asked. "Isn't that long enough to count?"

"No, no, no! You don't understand." Debbie was half laughing and half crying. "My family's been praying ever since I got a letter the first of the summer telling me you would be my roommate. We've been praying that you would be a Christian and not some wild party animal."

Debbie had been praying for my salvation the whole summer, though she didn't know me. God had used the prayers of people I didn't even know. I was amazed at the power of prayer and how God had brought us together.

That was the beginning of meeting many Christian friends from all walks of life-including good—looking football playes—who were involved in Fellowship of Christian Athletes®. Though I did lose some of my old friends because of my faith, God provided me many more Christian friends, who loved me unconditionally. I was surrounded by people who were committed to the Lord. Though I had once thought all committed Christians were nerds, I discovered how wrong I was—these were the coolest people I had ever met! I ended up with much better friends and much closer relationships than I had dreamed possible,

Once I settled into campus life, I found myself drawn to the girls in my dormitory who were especially troubled or depressed. Inevitably, they would end up in my room, where I would do my best to assist them. Since God had taught me to share my faith with Debbie, I now had the courage to talk about Christ with others. I found myself playing the roles of informal counselor and prayer partner. Although I had so recently become a Christian, people seemed to be drawn to me for help. I invited the girls to come to my prayer group to get them involved with Christians and lead them to a relationship with Jesus Christ.

The campus prayer group in which I was involved was simply called "the group," because we did not want any potential convert to be initially turned off by a religious label. It attracted Christians from different walks of life and different denominational backgrounds to work together for the Gospel.

I soon became a leader of "the group." I saw God working mightily through that college ministry. At my college in the early 1970s, I witnessed an incredible work of God among the students as denominational walls fell. College campuses across the country experienced an exciting time of revival as God liberally poured out His Spirit, and I had a great time being in the middle of it!

Staying on the Path

At the beginning of my freshman year in college, I still had no idea what I was supposed to do with my life. Nevertheless, I knew God had plans for me—plans for how I would serve Him. Since my life was now centered on Jesus Christ, though I wanted to find out what my future held, I no longer felt the same anxiety I had felt before I became a Christian.

In studying Scripture and praying for guidance, I ran across a passage in Proverbs that especially spoke to my heart: "Trust in the LORD with all your heart, and lean not on your own understanding; in all your ways acknowledge Him, and He shall direct your paths" (Prov. 3:5-6). Whenever I wondered what I was supposed to do with my life and what goals I should aim for, I reminded myself of that verse from Proverbs and remembered I needed to trust and obey. I could be confident that God would bring about His will for my life if I would just remain faithful to His Word.

The best way I know to describe my walk with the Lord at

that time—and even now—is to compare it to walking in the woods at night with a flashlight. In Psalm 119, it says that God's Word "is a lamp to my feet and a light to my path" (Ps. 119:105). Later in the same chapter, God promises to "direct my steps" by His Word (Ps. 119:133). These verses caused me to envision myself with a very small flashlight shining down on my feet. I had just enough light to put one foot in front of the other, taking one step at a time to follow the path I was on-trusting God that it would lead me where He wanted me to go. In my walk with the Lord, I had enough knowledge revealed to me in Scripture to be obedient to His will on a moment-by-moment, day-by-day basis—waiting patiently for Him to reveal my calling.

An Open Door

While studying in college and being involved with "the group," I had two vague ideas of what I might do in the future. I still considered some kind of sports career even though I could no longer play. I occasionally worked as an umpire, and I knew I could always be a coach. At the same time, because of my work in "the group" and in my dormitory, I felt called to try to help troubled young women, perhaps in a position of leadership.

The summer after my freshman year, God opened a door for me to be involved both with sports and with troubled girls. I was appointed by my state representative to work for Tennessee's correctional facility for juvenile delinquent girls. When my three-month internship was over, the assistant athletic director unexpectedly quit, leaving a vacancy that needed to be filled immediately. I was only eighteen years old, but was offered the job on the condition that I didn't let the girls know how young I was. The staff didn't want them to know I was only a little older than they.

Within two years I was promoted to the position of athletic director. That offer was also amazing because the position required a college degree, which I did not yet have. The state waived that requirement with the understanding that I was currently working toward my college degree in physical education.

I had known God would be faithful to meet my needs and plan my future. Still, I was overwhelmed by the way He opened a door to let me pursue both my desires.

2

The Growing Frustration
Working for the Government

There is a way which seems right to a man, but its end is the way of death. (Proverbs 14:12)

I glanced at my watch as I stood on the edge of the Olympic-sized pool. In only a couple minutes it would be time to get the girls out of the water and send them back to their dorms until morning. I wondered how they must feel, sleeping in small locked rooms on narrow metal beds, each room equipped with a toilet for nighttime necessities. It wasn't uncommon for housemothers to be attacked by girls who wanted to escape, so these were necessary precautions.

These girls were locked up for committing criminal offenses. Nevertheless, I cared deeply for them. I spent a lot of time praying for each girl to experience the love and forgiveness of Christ.

My job as athletic director was a dream come true. Besides the indoor pool in the same building as the full-sized gymnasium, the state institution provided outdoor tennis courts and basketball goals, a large softball field, a covered skating rink, a game room with vending machines, and the best athletic equipment money could buy. Most of the girls looked forward to recreation time, and I tried to make it as fun as possible. I was in charge of recreation and intramural competition, but my favorite responsibility was coaching the basketball, volleyball, and softball teams that competed in the city league off campus. My work was extremely challenging and I took my duties very seriously.

My two assistants were supervising another large group of girls in the gymnasium. Security required that the girls meet back in the gym and march, single file, back to their dormitories. Even with security guards looking on, girls would run for the fence, but not many had been successful in getting away. The guards usually caught up with them just as they were attempting to climb over the razor-sharp coiled barbed wire at the top of the fencing. Most of the time the girls were pulled off the fence with cuts, bleeding from being entangled in the wire. Such a failed attempt usually added a couple months additional time to their stay, and six weeks of solitary confinement in a small, dark room empty but for a tiny bed and toilet. I shuddered at the thought of it.

I blew my whistle to signal that it was time to get out of the pool. As they got out of the water and headed to the locker room to change, one of the girls dropped an envelope. By the time she realized she had lost it, I had picked the envelope up and opened it.

Inside was a marijuana cigarette. "Where did you get this, Lisa?" I asked her as she came toward me.

"Give it back to me," she said, as if I had stolen it from her.

I just shook my head. "Lisa, you know I can't give this back to you. Just go get dressed, and then we'll talk about it." I wanted to give Lisa the opportunity to get rid of the joint on her own, but knew I would have to write her up if she refused. If she had to go before the disciplinary committee she would have six weeks added to her time.

As Lisa headed toward the dressing room, I turned to make sure that all the other girls had gotten out of the water. A ball had been left floating in the pool, so I bent over the edge to retrieve it. I stood up and turned around, finding Lisa standing two feet in front of me with a softball bat she had grabbed out of the equipment room. She was so livid, her face was red with anger.

All the girls who had been in the pool were in the locker room getting dressed and my co-workers were in the gym next door. No one else was around—just Lisa and me.

As I faced this rather large, angry girl, I tried to look calm. Beneath my composure I was as scared as I had ever been.

"Lisa," I said loudly and firmly, not wanting her to sense the fear I was feeling, "you can knock me down with that bat and hurt me really badly, but the one who will ultimately end up being hurt is you. You know how much time that will add to your stay here."

Lisa glared at me, her eyes filled with hate, but she finally hesitated and started lowering the bat.

"You know you'll get in a lot more trouble if I write you up, so why don't we just throw the joint down the toilet and forget about it."

We walked to the restroom, and she threw it in the toilet, slowly reaching for the handle. I watched the joint swirling rapidly as the force of the water sucked it down the drain. I prayed a silent prayer thanking God for His protection.

A Government Education

I worked at the State of Tennessee correctional facility for delinquent girls for five years. Though the workers at the facility were required to carry mace for protection, I never needed to use it. Several other women workers were assaulted—one went to the hospital because a string cut into her neck when a girl tried to strangle her. But my confrontation with Lisa was the closest I came to being attacked.

God taught me many things while I was working for the State of Tennessee. These experiences enabled me to start Mercy Ministries. Nevertheless, most of my experiences with the government were heartbreaking. The times I was threatened by girls were not my worst experiences; the worst were the times I saw the broken lives of those girls getting worse at the facility instead of being restored.

"Nancy, you busy? I really need to talk to you about something." Carolyn, one of my co-workers was standing at the doorway of my office looking troubled.

"Sure! What's going on?"

"I'm afraid I have some bad news. Do you remember Lori?"

"Yes." I started to dread what I was about to hear.

"She's dead." Carolyn's voice was breaking as she told me what happened.

I looked at her—I didn't know what to say.

"When her mother found Lori, she was lying on the bathroom floor, dead from a gunshot wound to her head. She left a suicide note that said something about going to church for help, but that they wanted nothing to do with her. She simply requested to be buried in her jeans and T-shirt."

I was devastated.

Carolyn left me alone with thoughts of a conversation I had had with Lori a few days before her release to return to her hometown. Lori had experienced rejection throughout her life and she had no self-esteem. Severely abused from the time she was a small child, Lori tried to find fulfillment in lesbian relationships and hid behind a masculine appearance. I wanted to help Lori, but she erected an invisible wall to keep me and others from getting close. I had not been able to make her understand that God loved her.

The last time I saw her I gave her a Bible and pleaded with her to let me pray with her. When she refused, I advised her to find a church in her hometown where she could get spiritual help. I lived four hours from her hometown, and I was not familiar with the available churches in that city. But, I assured Lori that any church would help her if she would seek help.

I had no idea how the advice I gave Lori about finding a church would return to haunt me. For years I never told anyone about what happened because I felt personally responsible for her death.

Lori's case was so sad, so heartbreaking. She ended her life after being rejected at the very place where unconditional love should be constantly flowing. She received the best help the state had to offer, but without Christ there is no help.

The Gag Rule

After I found out about Lori's suicide, I became more determined than ever to share Christ with the girls in order to offer them genuine hope. I didn't want more girls to end up taking their own lives.

One day my co-worker Laura asked me, "Don't you think you need to tone down all this talk about Christianity?"

I looked at her, surprised. "What do you mean?"

"Well, I don't see how that's really going to help anybody."

I paused, looking to God for a way to answer her while trying to suppress painful memories of Lori that came to mind.

"Well, the way I look at it, sharing Christ isn't going to hurt anybody; and if it helps even one person, then it's worth it."

I developed a small library of Christian books in the gym that I encouraged the girls to check out and read. Many of these books were testimonies of young women who had become entangled in prostitution or drugs before their lives had been restored by Christ. The girls loved reading those books because they could relate to them. Many of the girls saw themselves as "hopeless cases," so when they read about the incredible conversions of young girls similar to themselves, they were encouraged. A few times I actually had to break up fights between girls who were arguing over who would get to read a certain book next. They would check out one book after another, devouring them from cover to cover.

The head of the correctional facility knew I was open with the girls about my faith in Jesus Christ. She said to me one day, "I don't mind your making Christian books available to the girls, or giving them Bibles. But if anyone ever complains about it, I'm going to have to talk to you." Thankfully, the entire time I worked as athletic director no one protested my attempts to introduce the girls to Jesus Christ.

I seldom saw any immediate results of my attempt to share the Gospel. I fought discouragement by reminding myself that God's Word will not return to Him void, but will accomplish what He sent it to accomplish (see Isa. 55:10-11). I prayed that the girls would meet other Christians who might build on what they had heard and lead them to the Lord. I reminded myself of the spiritual principle found in 1 Corinthians 3:7—that some plant, some water, but God gives the increase. I knew a lot of what I was doing in that place was seed planting so someone else could come along months, or perhaps even years, later and water the Word that was sown in their hearts. Above all I knew I was to be faithful with the opportunities I was given and trust God to bring the increase.

Occasionally, and excitingly, a girl would ask me privately to lead her in a prayer of salvation. So many of the girls had a hunger to know God and be taught spiritual principles for living a victorious Christian life. Sadly, however, these girls had no opportunity to be taught or discipled; thus they experienced very little, if any, spiritual growth. The fourth chapter of the Gospel of Mark describes how the sower sows the Word and immediately Satan comes to take away the Word that was sown in their hearts. It also describes how "the cares of this world, the deceitfulness of riches, and the desires for other things entering in choke the word, and it becomes unfruitful" (Mark 4:19).

In 1 Peter 2:2 new converts are instructed: "As newborn babes, desire the pure milk of the word, that you may grow thereby." In observing the girls who sincerely prayed the prayer of salvation then fell away, I understood what Peter was saying. As a newborn baby must have milk for nourishment in order to grow and survive, finally becoming strong enough for solid food, so must a newborn Christian have a steady diet of God's Word in order to grow into a mature believer.

Though these girls seemed like hard-core criminals, they were confused, hurting girls, many of whom had been victimized from the time they were born. Many had been victims of rape and incest, having been molested by fathers, stepfathers, brothers, and the boyfriends of their mothers, among others. Some had suffered severe neglect—abandoned and left wards of the state, shuffled in and out of foster homes and orphanages. Some had been trained by their mothers to be prostitutes.

Almost all the girls had had horrible things done to them, and many of them had also done horrible things. All of them had been sent to the facility by juvenile court judges. Some had been convicted of prostitution, breaking and entering, burglary, armed robbery, drug dealing and drug possession, and, in a few cases, murder.

The girls couldn't help but come to the correctional facility burdened by guilt from what they had done and by hatred toward those who had hurt them. Unforgiven and unforgiving, they carried a bitterness that affected every area of their lives. They desperately needed to forgive and to be forgiven. They desperately needed to discover that they could be set free from the guilt of all that they had done.

Yet no matter what kind of programs the government offers, no matter how many tax dollars it spends, and no matter how many experts it hires, the government cannot forgive their sin—not even one.

Only by the blood of Jesus can the stains of sin and guilt and shame be permanently removed. Only by being born again can a person leave the past behind and receive a new start in life. As the Apostle Paul so beautifully expressed, "Therefore if any man be in Christ, he is a new creature; old things are passed away; behold, all things are become new" (2 Cor. 5:17 KJV).

External conformity to the rules and regulations of the facility could not bring true change to the girls' lives. At best, the girls were merely prevented from doing bad things, while the desire for those things remained.

The best help the state institution could offer was what psychologists refer to as "behavior modification." By implementing a system of punishment and reward, outward behavior can be "modified." The results this produced were only temporary, however, and it was clear to me the girls cooperated so they could get out, but they remained the same on the inside. Once they returned to their same friends and environment, they began living as they had before. In many cases, the girls got in trouble and were sent back within a few weeks or months.

These girls needed transformation, *not modification*. God's ways are higher than man's. In Ezekiel 36:26-27 God revealed his plan to change mankind: "I will give you a new heart and put a new spirit within you; I will take the heart of stone out of your flesh and give you a heart of flesh. I will put My Spirit within you and cause you to walk in My statutes, and you will keep My judgments and do them."

God changes us on the inside! He gives us a new heart! He puts a new spirit within us! He takes our heart of stone and gives us a heart of flesh! God does not expect us to change ourselves by outward conformity to a set of rules—God changes our desires! We no longer want to sin; rather our desire is to please God. Paul put it this way when he wrote to the church at Philippi: "For it is God which worketh in you both to will and to do of his good pleasure" (Phil. 2:13 KJV). That is why Jesus said we must be born again—it is the only way to become a new person with old things passed away (see 2 Cor. 5:17); our transgressions are removed as far as the east is from the west (see Ps. 103:12). Likewise, when we accept Christ as Savior and receive forgiveness for our sins, they are removed from us as if we had never sinned. We have right standing with our Father God. Paul further explains in 2 Corinthians 5:21: "For he hath made him to be sin for us, who knew no sin; that we might be made the righteousness of God in him" (KJV).

This is the Good News—we can receive forgiveness; we can become brand-new persons! But someone has to tell those who do not know. "How then shall they call on him in whom they have not believed? And how shall they believe in him of whom they have not heard? And how shall they hear without a preacher?" (Rom. 10:14 KJV).

Looking Backward

Julie sat in front of the counselor's desk, fidgeting nervously. She dreaded hearing the results of the test she had taken.

Behind her desk, Mrs. Brandon, a psychologist for the state, looked over Julie's file without acknowledging the girl's presence. She did not want to speak until she had familiarized herself with Julie's past. There were so many girls in Mrs. Brandon's caseload that she was lucky if she recognized one of them by name, let alone remembered their case history.

Finally she looked up from the folder on her desk. "Julie, you're here to talk about your test results, aren't you?"

Julie nodded.

"According to what I have here, you were physically abused by your father roughly between the ages of four and eight. Is that right?"

"That's right," she answered, trying to suppress the painful images that rose unbidden from her memory.

"Also, according to what's written here, your father was abused by his father when he was a boy. Did you know that?"

Julie shook her head, looking puzzled. She wondered why her counselor was discussing her father's past with her. "What does that have to do with me?" she asked.

Mrs. Brandon smiled. "Julie, a person's behavior is determined by what they experienced in the past. Your father grew up in an abusive situation. His image of a father was one who mistreated his children. So, naturally, when he grew up and became a father, he fulfilled what he had learned by abusing his own children."

Julie started to get an idea of where Mrs. Brandon was headed and she did not like it.

"Now, if you should have children when you grow up," continued Mrs. Brandon, "it is extremely likely that you will abuse them just like you were abused by your father."

"You can't know that," objected Julie.

Mrs. Brandon adjusted her glasses and looked at her patient."How old are you, Julie?"

"Fourteen."

"Well, though I admire your desire not to repeat what's gone on in your family's past, I have to tell you, as someone who has studied these things for years and who has a degree in psychology, that your good intentions most likely will not prevent you from engaging in the same kind of behavior. Statistically speaking, I'm afraid you really don't stand much of a chance."

Julie is one of many girls I knew who, instead of being given hope for the future, was told that she could never escape the past. Government programs are not based on the message of the Gospel, but the message of modern psychology. This kind of counsel did great harm, because the girls were led to believe their future was determined by their past, and there was nothing they could do about it. This message of doom was based on personality profiles, case histories, and background studies. Many were told they would likely end up in prison, become abusive parents, or worse.

The girls were given no hope.

The teenage girls who heard the counselors' pronouncements were in no position to argue with trained psychologists. They accepted the message of "prophetic doom" they were given by the counselors who were supposed to be the experts. As a result, the statistical predictions became self-fulfilling prophecies. The Bible teaches that as a man "thinks in his heart, so is he" (Prov. 23:7). The girls were taught that they were products of their past—many believed the lie and acted accordingly.

The message given at the correctional facility was exactly opposite the message of the Gospel: "For I know the plans I have for you,' declares the LORD, 'plans to prosper you and not to harm you, plans to give you hope and a future.'" (Jer. 29:11 NIV). Because of the price Jesus paid, there is no need for the girls to be held in bondage to their pasts. They no longer have to be slaves to sin. "If the Son therefore shall make you free, you shall be free indeed" (John 8:36 KJV).

Environmental Pollution

Darlene was raised by her mother—she never learned who her father was. By the time she was fourteen, she had met a pimp and was involved in prostitution. He was able to provide her more security than she had in her broken home.

By age sixteen, Darlene was sentenced to spend a year in the correctional facility for soliciting. Her pimp was never charged due to a lack of evidence. Sadly this happens in most cases.

While at the facility, Darlene went through all the counseling and classes the government had mandated to be a part of the rehabilitation process. She stayed out of trouble and co-operated with the system to serve her sentences as quickly as possible.

Two years after she was released, we received word that Darlene had been murdered. Her pimp had involved her in a drug deal that went sour. Again I was reminded of the futility of trying to restore these girls apart from the hope that is in Christ. I couldn't help but think how different it could have been.

Darlene represents many girls who spent time at the correctional facility and returned to the same life-styles that had gotten them into trouble before. They were "doing time," conforming outwardly to rules and regulations in order to get out as soon as possible. They never really changed.

Not only were most of the girls destined to return to bad situations, but the environment of the correctional facility gave them a chance to learn the "tricks of the trade" from each other only to return to the streets and practice what they had learned. Additionally, lesbianism was common at the facility as it is in adult prisons. After leaving, many girls became involved in criminal activity again and, because they were no longer juveniles, were sentenced to the women's prison in Nashville.

The government has to do something about crime—it is necessary to have a place where juvenile offenders can be sent for committing criminal offenses. They need to know that there are consequences for the choices they have made. On the other hand, despite good intentions, it is impossible for anyone to be freed from their past apart from the delivering power of Jesus Christ.

Who Can Save?

At the beginning of Jesus' ministry. He proclaimed what was written about Himself in Isaiah:

> The Spirit of the Lord GOD is upon me; because the LORD hath anointed me to preach good tidings unto the meek; he hath sent me to bind up the brokenhearted, to proclaim liberty to the captives, and the opening of the prison to them that are bound. (Isaiah 61:1 KJV)

When people hear about troubled youths, runaways, teen drug users, and victims of physical and sexual abuse, they commonly assume that it is the government's responsibility to take care of them and restore their lives. Even Christians sometimes overlook their biblical responsibility, leaving it to the government.

The state cannot bring restoration to broken lives—it is unequipped for the task. The reason is simple: God has not anointed the government to "bind up the brokenhearted" or to "proclaim liberty to the captives." He has anointed the church. We are to set them free.

Though my five years at the correctional facility gave me

invaluable experience, they were also extremely frustrating years for me. One of the most significant lessons I learned was what *not to do* to help troubled girls.

Many of these girls thought God did not love them because of all the horrible things they had experienced. They needed to know that Satan, "the god of this world" (2 Cor. 4:4), was at work. He was the one bringing death and destruction to them, but Jesus came so we could have real life, abundant life. First John 3:8 says: "For this purpose the Son of God was manifested, that he might destroy the works of the devil" (KJV).

Only by Jesus, the name that is above every name, can the works of the devil be destroyed in the lives of people.

The system wasn't working. I did not feel I was contributing to any real improvement in the girls' lives. I had had a heavy dose of the government's way of dealing with all these problems—the results were disappointing.

I thought I might make a greater impact and see better results if I worked with a younger age group. Thus, I asked for and received a transfer out of Corrections and into the State Department of Human Services, working with children suffering from neglect and abuse. I felt that it might be possible to intervene in the lives of these children before they reached the point of being committed to a correctional facility. I hoped to become involved and see lives restored, but I was headed for even more frustration.

For the first year, I supervised foster care placements in the Nashville area. Then I had an opportunity for more challenging work with the Emergency Child Protective Services Unit. I was on call twenty-four hours a day, investigating charges of child abuse and neglect. Often my work would take me on a case with an investigative unit to a dangerous part of the city at any hour of the night. This position was challenging because it involved working with troubled youths and, though it was dangerous, it was also exciting.

One day I was sitting at my desk writing up case reports.

A few of my co-workers were in the room at their desks, also doing paperwork. We worked in a big room with many desks and big glass windows. Suddenly I heard a loud bang and glass flew around the room. A bullet had been fired through the window and had passed between a co-worker and me, hitting the opposite wall. We were only four feet apart. Though we never discovered the perpetrator of that drive-by shooting, we assumed it was an enraged parent whose child had been removed from the home because of abuse.

Another time, I responded to a report that a man had been physically abusing his children the previous night. Because it was broad daylight, I did not think I needed to arrange for a police escort. I found the house and went up and knocked on the door.

As I waited for a response, I wondered what I would find this time.

"Hi, I'm Nancy Alcorn from the Department of Human Services," I said, trying to sound pleasant. "We've had a report I'd like to discuss with you. May I come in?"

"Yes."

I immediately smelled the strong odor of alcohol on his breath. He was not stumbling drunk, but definitely under the influence. He slowly ambled over to his couch.

I sat across from him and I told him about the report we had received and that I would need to talk to his wife and children individually.

Suddenly the man's expression grew furious and he started yelling at me, "Nobody's going to take my children away from me!" As he shouted, his hand reached behind a pillow beside him and came out holding a revolver. "Get out of my house!"

Fear gripped me as thoughts of what could happen flooded my mind. But suddenly, a stronger force than fear took over. In a brief moment, my thoughts went to a Scripture in Psalm 91 where God promised to give His angels charge over me to protect me in all my ways of obedience and service. In a flash I knew everything was going to be okay.

"Sir," I said as calmly as I could, "I don't want to take your children away from you. If there's any possible way I can avoid that, I will. But if there is a problem, we want to help you. I am a Christian, and I care about people who need help. Jesus will help you if you ask Him to."

As I talked to the man about Jesus, his countenance softened, and he slowly put the gun on the couch and started crying. I said a silent prayer of thanks to God for His protection and intervention.

Because of the circumstances, we had to remove the children temporarily. However, as a result of this being handled with God's help, the man and his wife cooperated with us and agreed to receive the care and counsel offered by the state.

I had many other horrifying, traumatic experiences while I was with the investigative unit. One day around noon we received a call from the police to meet them at a sleazy hotel in downtown Nashville. They had received a report of someone possibly beating a child in one of the rooms, and I was assigned to check it out. I met two policemen at the hotel; they accompanied me upstairs.

They pounded on the door. "Police. Open up."

No one answered, but I could hear someone whimpering.

The police kicked open the door. I will never forget what I saw. In one corner, a man was crouching like a scared animal. The two officers cuffed him, leaving me to examine the little boy lying on the bed. He looked to be about seven years old. He was covered with blood and swollen from several lacerations on his face and upper body; he was shaking uncontrollably.

I bent over him and asked gently, "Can you tell me what happened?"

"Bad man beat me," he told me in a quaking voice. When he spoke, a tear slid down his cheek and mixed with his blood. He was obviously badly hurt, so we called an ambulance.

The boy's mother had gone out shopping and left him with her disturbed boyfriend. He had beaten the little boy with his fists and the heel of a shoe. The boy was admitted to the hospital for several days for a broken arm and cuts and bruises.

The state was able to repair the boy's arm, but I wondered who would fix the internal damage? Would he eventually grow up to abuse other children? I wished I could have the freedom to minister spiritually to such victims of abuse.

Another time I was beeped at home. A local hospital wanted me to come over right away. When I arrived, a doctor told me a woman had brought her eight-year-old girl to the emergency room with a broken leg. "There's absolutely no way this break could have occurred the way the girl's mother said it did," he said. "We need you to question her."

I talked to the mother in private and she adamantly stuck to her story. Finally I decided to speak from my heart. "Listen," I told her, "I am a Christian, and I understand that people do things sometimes because they're hurting and that they may need help themselves. If you'll tell me what really happened, I'll do my best to try to get help for you."

The woman began sobbing uncontrollably. When she regained her composure, she confessed to me that she had become so angry at her daughter that she had lost control. She propped her daughter's leg on the end of the couch and purposely broke it in two. A chill went down my spine as she told me what she had done—I could not imagine anyone doing such a thing.

Though the woman did get counseling from the mental health center, at the root of her violence lay a spiritual problem. No secular counseling program I knew of would be equipped to deal with the real spiritual issues underlying her behavior. There was no question in my mind that this woman was being driven by evil powers. Because of her desperation, I broke the rules and directed her to a pastor of a local church that was equipped to give her the right kind of help. By that time I had seen so many parents horribly abuse their children and then be disgusted by their own behavior that I was certain they were under the influence of evil spirits. Only the name of Jesus is above every name, and I knew in my heart that only the name of Jesus could set this woman free. It was my responsibility to take legal action against her by removing the child from her care, but my heart went out to her. I urged her to take the initiative to go to church and ask for spiritual help in addition to completing the required state counseling and psychiatric testing. I don't know what happened since I dealt with the emergencies and then turned the case over to a long-term counselor.

Another time I was called out late at night to go with police to a house neighbors had complained about. They reported that the house was so disgustingly filthy it was unfit for the two children living there. As two policemen waited outside, I went into the house and walked through it.

As I opened the front door, an unbearably foul stench hit me like a physical force. It was the filthiest place I had ever seen. Roaches and other insects crawled all over the walls, ceiling, and floors. A dog had had puppies on one of the beds and two weeks of refuse was dried up on the mattress. Insects had even invaded the refrigerator and freezer.

Though her two teenage children were extremely nice and seemed quite normal, the woman who lived there was oblivious to how repulsive her house was. I was overcome with what a horrible situation her children were being forced to live in. They were extremely embarrassed and ashamed, and I became incensed. "These kids are out of here tonight," I told the mother, "and I'm giving you three days to get this place cleaned up. No one should have to live in this much filth! I'll be back to check; and when I do, this place better be spotless."

I had avoided touching anything in the house. Nevertheless, when I came outside the waiting policemen spent several minutes examining me with a flashlight, picking off the roaches that had managed to get on my clothes and hair during my brief tour of the house. I shivered at the thought of a roach they might have missed crawling through my clothes.

That night I removed both of the teenagers for their own protection. Once again, however, I felt incapable of bringing restoration to the family. The woman's willingness to live in such a disgusting house was indicative of a much deeper, darker problem than any government program could possibly uncover. She must have disliked herself terribly to be willing to live in such utter filth. Only God could uncover the woman's deeply rooted problems that caused her to live this way.

I had many other experiences with degraded and broken lives. Such incidents caused me to feel the same frustration I had felt at the girls' correctional facility. I deeply desired to see the broken lives of those I was dealing with restored to wholeness. Instead I saw children being brought up in horrible situations with no hope of a new start in life. I saw cases of four-and-five-year-olds who were sexually molested by adults. It was heart wrenching.

The first five years of my state work, I was given an in-depth look at the teenage products of abuse, abandonment, neglect, and broken homes. The following three years, I was given an inside look at what small children experience growing up in abusive situations. God was showing me the whole picture—a sad picture—one that I will never forget.

As I reflected on the course my life had taken and my eight years of service with the State of Tennessee, I realized that God had purposely shown me the futility of trying to bring restoration to hurting humanity apart from the delivering power of the Gospel of Jesus Christ.

Looking back on it all, I now see that it was part of God's plan for me to *know* and *understand* that secular programs and secular treatment centers cannot produce lasting changes in the lives of people. They cannot forgive sin. They cannot heal broken hearts. They cannot restore shattered lives.

It was necessary for me to live out those eight years, regardless of the frustration, so that I would not be tempted to look to the wisdom of the world when I came up against difficult cases.

First Corinthians 1:19-20, states:

"I will destroy the wisdom of the wise; the intelligence of the intelligent I will frustrate." Where is the wise man? Where is the scholar? Where is the philosopher of this age? Has not God made foolish the wisdom of the world? (NIV)

No matter how many academic degrees a person may have, the real power to change a life is in the simplicity of the Gospel of Jesus Christ.

Although I was one of those people with degrees, I longed for the freedom to teach what I had learned in God's school. Even though I didn't realize it at the time, God was listening to the cry of my heart.

3

Stepping Out in Faith
The Beginning of Mercy Ministries

Now faith is the substance of things hoped for, the evidence of things not seen. But without faith it is impossible to please Him: for he that cometh to God must believe that He is, and that He is a rewarder of them that diligently seek Him. (Hebrews 11:1,6 KJV)

As I worked for the State of Tennessee and continued to deal with broken lives, I made a point of staying involved in my church. Without being involved in the life of the church, the sense of hopelessness and oppression that permeated my job would have been too overwhelming. I drew strength from knowing my pastors and several close friends prayed for me on a regular basis.

One day the associate pastor of my church called me. "Nancy, Teen Challenge has decided to open a home in Nashville, and they're holding a meeting with representatives from all the area churches.

"I've been praying about who should go on behalf of our church, and the Lord laid it on my heart to give you an opportunity to represent us. Are you interested?"

"Yes, I'm very interested," I replied. "I'd love to go." I was familiar with this ministry, founded by David Wilkerson, that helps troubled youth. Many of the books I had made available to the girls at the correctional facility were testimonies of teens whose broken lives had been restored through the Teen Challenge ministry.

All of us at that meeting were asked to briefly tell about ourselves and why we were there. Jimmy Lee, the head of Teen Challenge, had come from Chattanooga to set up the home and was intrigued by my experience with troubled girls. After the meeting we talked at length, sharing our experiences.

This initial meeting led to my involvement in the ministry. Jimmy invited me to attend a parent support group meeting he conducted weekly. The parents involved in this group all had rebellious children who had been involved in drugs, alcohol, and many other problems; some had committed crimes. Many of their children had been in and out of rehabilitation centers, only to return to their old habits again and again once they were released. Some of their children were currently in a Teen Challenge program getting help. Regardless of the specific circumstances, these parents needed help learning how to confront and deal with their children's problems.

The meetings would begin with Jimmy ministering from the Word to the desperate mothers and fathers. The parents would share the struggles they were having with their children and seek counsel from Jimmy. They also discussed what was going on in their own lives to learn how to better deal with their children. Many were taught about "tough love" for the first time. After a time of sharing and discussion, the group would pray for their children and for one another that they might be better parents.

One heartbroken man had a fifteen-year-old daughter named Debra who had run away from home; he didn't even know if she was still alive. The only thing that was keeping him going was the parents' group where he was given a sense of hope for his lost child.

It was an honor to be included in these meetings. Jimmy had the ability to give these parents a sense of hope by speak-

ing the Word of God and imparting to the group that God really was in control. Though their outward circumstances hadn't
changed, Jimmy taught them that through the power of
prayer, ultimately things *would* change as described in James
5:16, "Confess your faults one to another, and pray one for
another, that ye may be healed. The effectual fervent prayer of
a righteous man availeth much" (KJV). The group prayed fer-
vently, and things did change, just as God promised.

Jimmy also shared testimonies of how other teenagers,
whose lives had been ravaged by the same kinds of problems,
had been restored when they gave their lives to Christ and
were saturated in God's love. In every case, the changes that
had occurred in these teens' lives had resulted from relying on
the Word and continuous prayer.

Through these meetings I learned how to deal with the parents and their pain, which was a new experience for me. I also
learned more about dealing with the children themselves, and
specifically counseling from a Christian perspective. Not only
was it a tremendous education, it was also very exciting to see
the positive results.

Eventually, Jimmy asked, "Nancy, in your free time would
you be interested in working with girls who come to us for
help? We're not in a position to hire staff at this time, but I
know you have a heart for these girls and their problems, and
I could really use your help."

His question wasn't difficult for me to answer. I jumped at
the opportunity!

That was the beginning of a volunteer relationship with
Teen Challenge that lasted over a year. I started working with
one or two girls a week. As the number of girls increased,
Jimmy asked me to keep track of my hours so that he would
know how much time I was devoting to Teen Challenge. I
bought a personal log book and found that eventually I was
working almost as much for the ministry as I was for the state.

The girls who came to Teen Challenge for help and counseling had the same kinds of problems and broken lives as those I had worked with in the correctional facility. But there was an obvious difference between the kind of help they were receiving through the Christian-based Teen Challenge program as opposed to the state-run program. I was seeing dramatic results in the lives of the girls who had embraced Jesus as their Master and Savior, while those who had been left to the methods of the "system" had continued down their hopeless paths.

The federal government conducted a major research project on the contrast between the results achieved by Teen Challenge and other Christ-centered programs versus secular programs. The research showed that although both the Christ-centered and the secular programs had some similarities, the Christian programs had a success rate of over eighty-seven percent, compared to less than three percent for secular programs. The only major, identifiable difference between the two was the inclusion of teaching Christian values. A film titled "The Jesus Factor" was produced which dramatically portrayed the differences.

I continued to attend the support group and pray with the parents. One night the man whose daughter had been missing came to the meeting with news that she had been found in another state and arrested for prostitution. She would be returned to Tennessee. That night we thanked God that Debra was alive and coming home and we prayed for her restoration. At the next meeting her father reported that she had been sentenced to spend a year in the correctional facility where I had worked.

Although he had hoped Debra could come home, she had broken the law and her father understood that Debra would have to pay the penalty. We did our best to reassure him, but I wished there had been an alternative.

I'd been working as a volunteer with Teen Challenge while continuing with the state for about a year when I was offered a job with a ministry based in Illinois called Team Thrust for the Nations. Team Thrust's focus was ministering to street people in large cities. Convinced that the state was not equipped to restore broken lives, I had been looking for an opportunity to leave my position with Human Services.

I was impressed with the work Team Thrust was doing and wanted to get involved in a situation where I could share the Gospel full-time. Reverend Eddie Cunningham, founder of Team Thrust, had worked with street people and the homeless for years, and I knew I could learn a lot from him. His wife, Lonnie, had previously directed the New Life for Girls home in Mississippi, and I knew I could benefit from her experience as well. I took the job with the understanding that it would be a temporary situation.

Working with Team Thrust I was trained to do street ministry in New York City and a few other metropolitan areas. During that time, God brought me face-to-face with the plight of street people. These homeless, nameless faces were often addicted to alcohol and drugs and lived like animals in the filth of the city. They ate out of garbage cans, slept in cardboard boxes, and begged for money. I learned from many of the homeless that they had grown up in the same kind of environment as the girls I had worked with at the state facility. Again I longed to work with troubled girls in a Christian environment so they would have a chance to live joyful, fulfilling lives and not end up on the streets.

Through my experiences reaching out to these people, the Lord continued to put a burden on my heart to help hurting humanity His way. My training with the Cunninghams, though brief, was invaluable, and it further strengthened my desire to follow God's direction for my life.

I had been working with Team Thrust for about six months when Jimmy Lee called. Nashville Teen Challenge was now able to hire a full-time staff person—they wanted me to be their director of women. With the full blessing of Eddie and Lonnie, I accepted the position and moved back to Nashville.

Working for Teen Challenge was answered prayer. God knew the desire of my heart was to work with troubled girls, and He also knew how painful it had been for me with the state, where I saw no lasting results. I was finally being given the opportunity to reach out to these girls in a Christian environment through the Teen Challenge program. God had opened the door for me and I could see how He had ordered my steps along the way.

By the time I started working for Teen Challenge as a full-time employee, we had been given a house to be used as the home for the girls. It needed some repairs and other work before it could be opened, so I continued to counsel girls in the office until the work could be completed.

I also resumed attending the parents' support group meetings. By this time, Debra had been in the correctional facility seven months. The parents had continued to pray for her every week. One evening after a meeting I asked Debra's father, "Wouldn't it be great if after she finished her sentence, Debra could come to the Teen Challenge home? It should be open by then." He thought it was a wonderful idea but wasn't sure he could convince her to go and asked if I would consider contacting her.

I wrote Debra a letter describing the home we were planning to open. I asked if she would be interested in getting spiritual help and making a new start in life. She wrote back that she was interested and asked me for more information.

I wanted to talk to Debra face-to-face, so I called the facility and asked if I could visit her to talk about the Teen Challenge home. Not only was I given permission to see Debra, but I was asked to make a presentation about the ministry to all the girls in case others were interested.

As I walked across the grounds of the correctional facility, the memories of my experiences and my frustrations working in that godless environment flooded my mind as though I had just left yesterday. As a staff member, I had always felt so helpless, unable to offer the girls anything substantial to permanently change their lives for the better.

Now, three years later, I had been given the opportunity to come back and freely share the vision of hope that was available to these girls through the Christ-centered program of Teen Challenge. I quickened my step as I neared the auditorium, feeling the power of God in my spirit.

When I finally met Debra in person, I was not prepared for what I saw. She was absolutely beautiful and had a look of innocence. Though she was lovely on the outside, there was a hardness and bitterness about her. She desperately needed Jesus in her life, just like all the other girls in the facility.

She said she was eager to come to the home — so eager, in fact, that she asked if I thought I could pull some strings to get her released early.

Although I felt she was sincere about wanting to come to the home, I'd worked with dozens of girls like Debra and knew she was trying to manipulate me a little. Part of me wanted to see if I could get her out, but I knew it was important that she serve out her time.

"If you're as sincere about coming to Teen Challenge in five months as you are now, that will be soon enough," I replied. "You need to finish your time here, and once you're released you can come to the home, but you should be sure you're coming for the right reasons."

Although she was disappointed, she seemed to understand, and she recognized that she couldn't con me.

The parents' group was pleased to hear that Debra was committed to coming to the home. We all felt it would only be a matter of time before she committed her life to Christ. Her father was extremely encouraged by what I reported and agreed that she needed to finish her time in the correctional facility before entering the Teen Challenge program.

The Teen Challenge home opened about the same time Debra was released, in the fall of 1981. She was brought to the home by staff from the correctional facility. As I watched the state vehicle pull up in the driveway, I had a sense of having come full circle. It seemed so ironic that the first girl to come to the home was coming from the same place where I had labored in vain for so many years trying to make a difference. I had dreamed of the day I could work with girls, teaching the love of Jesus Christ from God's Word so that they could have a total transformation from the inside out. I had experienced so much frustration watching those girls being held captive in that juvenile prison because I knew they were prisoners to far more than bars and barbed wire. The moment Debra stepped from the car. God confirmed in my spirit that He would bless the work I did in Him and that He would set the captives free. One week after arriving at the home Debra committed her life to Christ and had a desire to allow Him to change her into His image.

It was decided that I would live in the home with the girls. We had room to accommodate one staff person and six girls, and we were always full. I also counseled dozens of girls who didn't reside at the home, sometimes placing them in other Teen Challenge homes around the country.

Though I cared deeply for the girls and was excited about the progress they were making, they sometimes tried my patience. One day Debra made me so frustrated with her rebellious attitude that I literally backed her up against a wall and got right in her face. "Debra," I yelled, "if you're not willing to abide by the rules like everyone else, then you don't need to be here!" I called her father and asked him to come get her. However, by the time her dad arrived, Debra and I had talked and prayed, and God convicted me that it was not His will for her to leave.

I apologized for losing my temper and said she could stay, but felt it necessary that she be disciplined for her rebellion. In order for her to remain at the home, I told her she must agree to wash every single dish, including knives, forks, and spoons, for the entire household, after every meal, for a solid week! This was a strong punishment, but Debra agreed to do it because she sincerely wanted to change and do the right things to improve the way she lived.

This incident was a turning point for Debra. Her attitude improved dramatically and her commitment to serve God became even stronger. In fact, she never rebelled again during her time in the home.

An important part of the girls' spiritual growth was to become actively involved in fellowship with the body of Christ. It was critical to establish this involvement while they were in the home so they would be rooted and grounded in God once they left the home. We were frequently invited to participate in local church activities.

One time we attended a weekend retreat with a youth group. The girls and the members of the youth group were all about the same ages so there was a lot of camaraderie. During the retreat, Debra met a handsome young man named Steve. Debra had never met a guy her age who had such strong spiritual commitments; they were inseparable all weekend.

The weekend went so well that we started attending the youth group on a regular basis. Debra continued to grow stronger in the Lord and saw Steve when we attended the youth activities. A few months after their first meeting Debra graduated from Teen Challenge. Not long after graduation, Steve and Debra married and moved to Virginia Beach, Virginia. She and Steve have two children and have moved back to Nashville. They rejoined the church where they originally met and became active members.

The life of this one girl is representative of the kind of transformation that occurred over and over when the power of the Word and the loving forgiveness of Jesus were presented. Jesus doesn't only *make* the difference, He *is* the difference.

Teen Challenge was a critical stepping-stone in my life commitment to ministry. I had the opportunity to direct the outreach in Nashville, and I also received valuable training from other Teen Challenge homes whose programs were already established. I learned a great deal working with experienced people like Jimmy Lee, and some of my greatest lessons were taught by the girls themselves.

I also know I made a lot of mistakes while I was with Teen Challenge. Looking back, I can see that my spiritual maturity during that time was not adequate for the task, but God had placed me there. He made clear to me that although humans look at the outward appearance, He looks at the heart. God knew my heart and He knew what I could be in Him. I had no idea how powerful and meaningful those lessons would become.

Living on a Prayer

I had been with Teen Challenge for about eighteen months when some close friends of mine moved to Monroe, Louisiana. They had been very supportive of me and my work in the ministry. In fact, they volunteered at the home on a regular basis, teaching Bible classes and sharing with the girls.

I was sad when they left, but they promised to invite me to visit them once they got settled. Sure enough, not long after they moved I got an invitation to spend a week with them. Though I loved working with the girls, living at the home twenty-four hours a day was sometimes draining. Looking forward to a much needed break, I headed south.

During the week I was in Monroe, I accompanied my friends to church, attended Bible studies, and enjoyed other times of fellowship. I had many opportunities to share about my work at Teen Challenge and the miracles taking place in the lives of the girls. In response, nearly everyone I talked to commented on how good it was to hear about a program for teens that was really working. They shared with me about the growing drug and alcohol problems among the teens in their community. Sadly, there was no place like Teen Challenge in the entire state, but the need was certainly present.

When the week ended, I had met many fine people in

Monroe and thoroughly enjoyed my visit. I left, promising to visit again.

Although I was glad to get back to Nashville, it seemed as though a little of Monroe came home with me. I couldn't get those conversations about the need for a home off my mind. I dismissed the thoughts for a while because I loved what I was doing and had no desire to leave Nashville.

When the thoughts and feelings persisted, I began to diligently pray, asking the Lord if He was trying to show me something. After several weeks of prayer, the Holy Spirit made clear that I was being called to raise up a home in Louisiana.

Although I didn't doubt that I was being called, I still sought the counsel of several Christian advisers whose spiritual wisdom and discernment I respected. Through them and in other ways, God reinforced to me that I was to go in faith to Monroe and that He would be my provider.

I considered the possibility that I was supposed to go and start a new Teen Challenge home. However, the Lord had planted in me the knowledge that He was going to broaden the vision. Though I knew I was to continue working with troubled girls, in my heart I knew that eventually the ministry would also encompass reaching out to unwed mothers.

I talked to my supervisor about this new calling and the possibility of opening a Teen Challenge home in Monroe that would include an outreach to pregnant teens. He was very understanding and supportive, but he told me that the vision of Teen Challenge did not include work in that area of ministry.

I also took my vision to the board of Teen Challenge. They accepted my resignation and sent me off with their blessing. My supervisor, the staff at Teen Challenge, and several board members and close friends of the ministry gave me a going away party and presented me with a check for a thousand dollars to get settled in Louisiana. This was the first sign God gave me as confirmation of His provision.

As I was finalizing my plans to move to Monroe, I knew I needed to tell my family.

"I have a new job opportunity in Monroe, Louisiana," I told them. "I plan to leave in three weeks."

Unsure whether to be happy or concerned, they hesitated to reply. "Well, what kind of job is it?" my mother asked.

"It's pretty similar to what I'm doing now."

"Do they already have a home started?"

"I'll be helping to raise one."

"How much does it pay?"

That was a tough one. "Well, I'm not really sure exactly."

"You don't know what your new job is going to pay?" my mother inquired, looking a little worried.

The direct answer to that question was that I had no idea what my income would be. I didn't want to worry my parents, but God had given me the assurance that I would eventually be more blessed if I would go to Louisiana. So I simply said, "Well, we haven't settled on a definite amount yet, but I know I'll be making more than I am now."

I knew I was "stretching" it a bit, but I had learned from God's Word to "calleth those things which be not as though they were" (Romans 4:17 KJV), and I was speaking in faith what God had spoken to my heart.

Before I left Nashville, God impressed on me two specific things that I must faithfully do to experience His provision both personally and for the ministry. First, God showed me that I must tithe on all the contributions given to the ministry just as I tithed on my personal income. He made it clear that the sowing and reaping principles that apply to personal giving are just as applicable to the giving of a ministry.

Second, God showed me that I was not to charge the girls who came to the home, but to freely minister to their needs. It was important for these girls to know that we were not motivated by money to reach out to them, but rather by the unconditional love of Jesus Christ. The Lord convicted me that if I remained faithful in these small things, I would never lack and neither would the ministry.

I'd learned a great deal about faith, especially during my two years at Teen Challenge. God had honored each step of faith I had taken to this point, and I trusted Him completely. I knew this was a turning point, a new adventure and challenge God had placed before me. But now He was asking that I take a leap of faith, calling me to His work in Louisiana without a job, a place to live, or the security of a paycheck. I was excited that He had called me to raise up this home, but I was also overwhelmed.

The hardest part about going to Louisiana was leaving my life in Nashville. I was very involved in my church, had many friends, and my family lived nearby.

I remember breaking the news to a close friend at lunch one day. I told her about all the events that had led to my decision. I explained to her that God had shown me that my obedience to Him would bring much fruit and that He had assured me of His provision for my life. I admitted that I had some apprehension not knowing what lay ahead.

"But, Kathy," I told her, "if I'm truly hearing from God, and I believe I am, He has made clear to me that when I raise up His work, the lives of many will be saved."

Kathy looked at me for a long time after I finished talking before she responded.

"Nancy, the whole time you were talking, I kept hoping you weren't going to tell me that you are moving to Monroe. But I know by what you've shared with me that you must go. Selfishly, I want you to stay, but there's no way I can refute what you've shared with me. I can see God in this so clearly and He definitely has big plans for you!"

After many tearful good-byes, I left Nashville in January 1983, drove to Monroe, and found an apartment. Between moving expenses, rent, and other obligations, the thousand dollars Teen Challenge had given me was gone by the second month. All I could do was believe for God's provision.

Immediately after arriving in Monroe I became involved in a local church and several Bible studies. Through my involvement with Christians in Monroe and those in Nashville who knew I had gone in faith, the Lord raised support for me. I was never lacking in food, clothing, shelter, or the ability to meet my other obligations. Even though I never told people about my pressing needs, I would frequently receive money from someone just when I needed it.

The second month I was in Monroe, I received a check for five hundred dollars the same day my rent and utilities were due — an amount that added up to well over four hundred dollars.

Occasionally, I would go a day with an empty refrigerator, but inevitably someone would knock on my door with either money or a bag of groceries. The person standing at my door would often appear rather awkward, either unsure as to whether he or she was doing the right thing or concerned that I might be embarrassed. "Nancy, I hope you don't mind," the person would say, "but I felt prompted to bring this to you."

I always assured them that they had indeed heard from the Lord and that their gift was timely and was meeting a definite need. I was overwhelmed at God's faithfulness to do exactly what He said He would do. God impressed on me that if I pleased Him, He would see that my needs would be met as His Word promised: "But my God shall supply all your need according to His riches in glory by Christ Jesus" (Philippians 4:19 KJV).

The Unfolding of the Vision

"You actually think you can make this work? How are you going to operate?"

The mayor of West Monroe, Louisiana, was sitting at his desk across from me, looking puzzled. I had been telling him about the home I wanted to establish in his city.

"I'm sure God sent me here to do this and that He will provide for us," I replied, hoping my enthusiasm would be contagious.

"And you think you can run your home without taking any form of government aid—no state, federal, or at least parish assistance? Without even applying for aid from the city?" The mayor appeared skeptical.

"If we take government funds, we won't have the freedom to share Christ and teach biblical principles. Unless we are able to immerse these troubled girls in the truth, we won't have a chance to affect any lasting changes in their lives. Having worked for the State of Tennessee for eight years and witnessing firsthand how little those programs were able to bring about any permanent changes, I know what I'm talking about."

The mayor seemed to understand my dilemma but asked, "How much will you be charging these girls to come to your home?"

"We're not going to charge them anything," I replied. "God showed me that I am to operate in the unconditional love of Christ by allowing these girls to come free of charge. In this way they will know that we really care and that we're not trying to make money off their problems."

The mayor just looked at me. Finally, he said, "I think what you want to do is a wonderful idea and I wish you well, but..." He let his sentence trail off into silence.

It was obvious he did not think for one minute the ministry would get off the ground. I didn't blame him. It was all I could do to keep myself from being discouraged as I walked out of his office.

Despite occasional doubts that tried to press on my mind, God continued to be faithful. He arranged for me to share the vision with others in some profound ways. After I had been in Monroe just two months, I received a phone call from the editor of the local newspaper. A mutual friend had told him about my coming to Monroe to start a home for troubled girls.

"Would you be willing to come to my office and be interviewed for a story?" he asked.

"Sure," I agreed eagerly.

He interviewed me in-depth and had my picture taken, but he gave me no idea how much of the information he planned to use. I was quite surprised—and pleased—that the entire front page of the second section of the paper was devoted to my purpose for coming to Monroe. The article was accompanied by a gripping sketch of a child with a tear running down his face. I was amazed by how God had worked to publicize the vision of bringing restoration to broken lives.

The article outlined my experiences working for the State of Tennessee and Teen Challenge and gave a detailed accounting of my purpose for coming to Monroe. It described the home I planned to start for troubled girls and ended by recommending that local organizations invite me to speak. As a result, I began to receive numerous invitations to present the vision to local churches and civic groups.

As I spoke before different groups, people began to make monthly commitments to help establish the home. The Lord also opened doors for me to meet prominent people in the Monroe area who wanted to help.

I began to prayerfully select people for the advisory board who shared the vision of restoring broken lives. This board consisted of businessmen and women representing a cross-section of Christians from many denominations. It was especially exciting to see the churches unite despite denominational differences. The ministry was taking shape, and we had many needs. The board and I came together as one body in Christ and prayed for these needs to be met.

One of our most pressing needs at that time was for office space so a part-time secretary and I would have a place to work. It was also one of the first prayers God answered for us. A local realtor learned of our need; he telephoned offering to donate a large office building for us to use as long as we needed it.

At that point, eight months after I had come to Louisiana, the board voted to give me a modest salary. Though it was not nearly as much as I had made in the past, God would prove to me that He was my source and not the size of my paycheck. He provided for me personally by moving the hearts of others to supply my needs.

One morning, for example. Dr. Rabun Smith, a Monroe dentist, came into my office. "I just dropped by for a visit," he said, smiling. "I wanted you to know I'm really excited about what you're doing here."

"Thank you very much," I said sincerely. I was always pleased to get positive feedback from Christians in the community.

"By the way, the Lord's been talking to me about some kind of car payment that you have. Do you have a car payment?"

"Yes, sir."

"How much is it?"

I told him the amount of my monthly payment.

"No, I don't mean how much a month. I mean how much do you still owe on your car?"

"I think it's between forty-five and forty-six hundred."

"Well, I believe God's been telling me I'm supposed to help you with that." He pulled out his checkbook and began writing. "Now this is not for Mercy Ministries; this is for *you*," he said, handing it to me.

As I stared at the check, I was speechless. It was for forty-six hundred dollars.

Dr. Smith grinned and said, "Now go pay off your car."

Through experiences like this the Lord continued to fortify my trust and faith in Him to meet all my needs as well as those of the ministry.

Once our advisory board was established, we decided it was time to spread the word further about Mercy Ministries. We printed brochures that described the home we were planning to open and listed the names of the board members.

Jim and Kathy Edwards, friends in Nashville who owned a direct mail company, graciously offered to donate their services to the ministry. They obtained a list of approximately

20,000 Monroe-area residents and sent them our brochure along with a letter from me.

Although few people who received that mailing had heard of Mercy Ministries or me, many of them knew or were familiar with one or more members of our advisory board. People who had received our mailing began calling our board members at home to get more information about Mercy Ministries. The board members would describe our vision in detail and explain why they had chosen to become involved. God was able to work through our board to motivate people to contribute. Through our ongoing mailings and contact with these people, many of them befriended the ministry and started giving regularly.

As Mercy Ministries became better known, I began to receive invitations to speak at public schools. The schools were strict about keeping religion out, but they knew I was always outspoken about the Gospel, so this was a unique opportunity.

The principal of one school told me, "I'm not supposed to let you talk about God."

Although I knew this was true, I was not prepared to talk about anything else. As I began to tell him how important it was that I be able to share with the students what a difference God could make in their lives, he interrupted me.

"I'm going to leave you here to speak and I'm going back to my office. When you're done, you can come find me. That way if anyone complains to me that you spoke about Jesus in the classroom, I can honestly say I didn't hear it." As he walked away, my heart was full of gratitude knowing that God still had His people in positions of authority in our public school system, people who understand that there is only one message that can truly make a difference in the future of all those kids.

He left me alone in the auditorium, and I told the students the message of hope they needed to hear.

Thereafter, I spoke in public schools on many occasions.

One school, which was aware of the miraculous results being achieved in the lives of the girls who had come to us for help, required any student who was given a three-day suspension to come to the Mercy Ministries office for counseling.

Still holding to our commitment not to receive state or federal funding, the Lord honored our obedience. However, we still couldn't afford a home and had not been able to find the right place. And because so many people had now heard about us, we were receiving calls from more and more girls seeking help. We prayed daily, believing God would provide the property and an appropriate house.

One Saturday I met with two friends to pray for the provision of a home. After our meeting, I stopped at a gas station to fill up my car. As I was pulling away, something inside of me said, "Go get a newspaper." I almost ignored the impulse but decided that God must be trying to tell me something. I got a newspaper and turned to the real estate section.

The last advertisement I came to caught my attention. It described a large house with many bedrooms, a large recreation room, a pool and pool house, and a privacy fence surrounding the premises; yet the price was extremely low. I looked at the house that night—it was better than I could have possibly hoped. Because it was a few feet outside the city limits, no zoning laws applied. It was perfect!

The house was owned by a man and his large family who lived next door to his elderly mother. As he had prospered he had added to his home several times instead of moving because he wanted to look after his mother. As a result, he overbuilt his house for the neighborhood and he could not recover his cost.

That Saturday evening I was so excited about the house I could barely wait to show the board members on Monday. When they saw it, they joined me in my excitement. It was obvious to all of them that this was the perfect home for Mercy Ministries.

"There's only one problem," one of the board members spoke up, "we don't have the money."

"That's not a problem," I replied, smiling. "We just need to sign the purchase agreement and trust God to provide the funds within the thirty days before closing. He's found us the right home. He'll find us the money to pay for it.

"During that time we can let the people who have expressed interest in Mercy Ministries know what we're doing and give them an opportunity to help. I have a list of people I've met at speaking engagements who asked to be contacted when we're ready to build. Let's get in touch with them and tell them we've found a home that's perfect for our needs priced far below the cost of building a new one. We'll also let them know we have a deadline."

We talked about it for a while and agreed in prayer that we should sign the purchase agreement and trust God to direct us in raising the money.

A few days after we signed the agreement, Dr. Smith came to me with three board members—Jerry Hightower, Bill Husted, and Susan Cordell—and offered their help.

"Nancy," they said, "we'd like to introduce you to all the businesspeople we know in the area so you can share your vision with them. We think they might want to help you raise the money to buy the home."

"That's great!" I exclaimed. "Let's go for it!"

During the next thirty days the four of them introduced me to numerous businesspeople with whom they had established relationships over the years. God moved both Christians and non-Christians to offer substantial contributions to Mercy Ministries. The size of their gifts varied, but the average donation was about three thousand dollars. At the end of the thirty days, we had two-thirds of the money in cash. To make up the difference, one of the members of the board graciously volunteered to sign a short-term loan.

With the money we received and the loan (which was paid

off within a year) we bought our first home. The gentleman who sold us the house was pleased with how we were planning to use it. I assured him we would take good care of his home and check on his mother regularly.

Now that we owned the home we were ready to begin renovating it to meet our specific needs. We put the word out to different churches from all over the Monroe area. People from all denominations responded, coming together for several workdays in which we cleaned and painted the house. So many people were willing to help that we had to eat lunch in shifts from a huge pot of chili. Not only did a great deal of work get accomplished, but we had a wonderful time of fun and fellowship as well.

Our First Girl

The paint was barely dry when we started getting calls from girls needing help. In less than a month the house was full of girls with various problems. We shared with each the unconditional love of Jesus Christ and led her in a prayer of salvation. A routine was established to include a daily schedule of devotion, Bible teaching and spiritual guidance, individual counseling, meal preparation and cleanup, recreational time, and other activities and responsibilities.

Many miracles occurred in the lives of these girls as they accepted Jesus Christ as their personal Savior. The Lord literally transformed them before our eyes.

I'll never forget the first girl who came to Mercy Ministries. Our office received a call from someone who had a friend in need of our help.

"Her name is Theresa," the caller said. "She's nineteen years old and is heavily involved in drugs and alcohol. We're very worried about her because she's been depressed lately and has attempted suicide in the past. We heard about the home you're starting and were wondering if you could help her. We asked Theresa if she would be willing to talk to you, and she said she would if you called her."

The caller gave me Theresa's phone number and address, and I assured him I would call her immediately.

When Theresa answered the phone, her speech was heavily slurred. I managed to find out that she was alone, but I couldn't really decipher anything else she said. I was concerned because of her suicide attempts and decided to go see her to make sure she was all right.

A volunteer and I drove to Theresa's house. We knocked on the door repeatedly but got no answer. Since I had called only a few minutes earlier it was unlikely that she had left. Through a window on the side of the house we saw Theresa lying on the living room floor.

Finding a door that was unlocked, we went into the house. Theresa was still conscious, but incoherent. We were able to get her up and help her walk to my car. At the emergency room her stomach was pumped and she was required to stay in the psychiatric ward for three days of observation.

While Theresa was in the hospital, we reached her parents who provided more details about her. They were at the end of their rope, not knowing what they could do to help her. They were eager for her to go to Mercy Ministries, and Theresa was willing to come.

The hospital released her and she came directly to the home. Theresa had had time to think about the mess she had made of her life and how near she had come to death. She was scared and she wanted our help. We told her Jesus had a purpose and a plan for her life and that all she needed to do was ask Him into her heart and He would forgive her and cleanse her of her past. She responded immediately and prayed the prayer of salvation for her life.

We taught Theresa and the other girls about the ways of God and how to apply His Word in their lives to help them grow spiritually. We wanted them to learn a whole new way of life and how to continue to live as Christians once they left the home. We wanted to make them disciples, not just converts.

Theresa did well at Mercy Ministries and was eager to apply the principles we taught her. She graduated from the program "a new creature in Christ" and continued attending a local church. Initially she stayed in close contact with us, stopping by the home or calling. She started dating a young man who was a new Christian and she brought him by to meet us, but we didn't hear from her again for several months.

About a year later Theresa called to tell us her boyfriend had committed suicide. He had started having problems with his past and had been under a lot of pressure, but no one had any idea how depressed he had become. Theresa loved this man and was devastated by his death. She understood first-hand the hopelessness that can drive someone to take his or her own life.

Despite the help we tried to give Theresa, the death of her boyfriend was more than she could handle, and she fell back into her old way of life. She eventually came to us for counseling to get her life back on track. We prayed with her and told her that God would heal her broken heart and that Jesus bore her grief so she wouldn't have to. We also told her it was important for her to trust God and try to go on with her life. There was nothing she could do to bring back her boyfriend's life, but she had a choice about her own. Through the counseling she decided to go to nursing school, and we encouraged her in this decision.

After Theresa left for nursing school we did not hear from her again, and I often wondered what happened to her.

A couple years later I was visiting one of the members of our staff who had been hospitalized for tests. As I was sitting there in my friend's hospital room, a nurse came in. We immediately recognized each other—it was Theresa! She looked great and it was exciting to see her standing there in her uniform.

She told me she had graduated from nursing school and she loved her work. It hadn't been easy and she was still struggling in a few areas but was living a Christian life. I was overjoyed to discover that Theresa had not fallen away from her commitment to Christ but was holding down a steady job and had a stable life.

The Expanding Vision

A steady stream of girls continued to come to the home from all over Louisiana and then from all over the United States. We were filled to capacity and often had a waiting list. There were trying times as people came to work on staff and decided a few months later it was not their calling. Nevertheless, the Lord sustained us.

Although our finances were often tight, God remained faithful in meeting our needs. Sometimes the help would come at the last minute. One day we needed to deliver a check to the electric company by the end of the day to prevent them from cutting off our electricity. We had been praying and believing for the money, but the deadline was just hours away and we were trying not to give in to worry. Though we had no idea where the money was going to come from, we knew God would provide it and it was important for us to trust Him.

However, time kept ticking by. Noon came and went. I stayed busy, trying not to give in to doubt and unbelief.

About four that afternoon there was a knock on the door. A gentleman who had become a frequent supporter was standing on the front steps, looking a little unsure of himself.

"Hello," he said. "I'm sorry to bother you like this. I was about to mail this check to you, but something seemed to be telling me, 'Don't put it in the mail; take it there yourself.'"

"You heard right!" I exclaimed. "Now, let me have that check, I'll explain to you later." The check made it to the electric company in the nick of time.

That was only one of many times it seemed impossible to meet our financial obligations. God did not simply allow us to survive; He caused us to grow.

Jim and Kathy Edwards continued donating their direct

mail services, which allowed us to keep in touch with our prospects and contributors on an ongoing basis. As a result, more people became regular contributors. As God brought restoration to the broken lives of the girls who came to Mercy Ministries, I started including the stories of these miraculous changes in the thank-you letters we sent to our contributors. We wanted them to know how their faithful financial support was enabling us to help girls get back on track.

We got invitations from all over Louisiana to share the stories of how God was using Mercy Ministries to help troubled girls. Many times, I brought one or two of the girls with me to tell their stories. Before long, speaking invitations came from other states as well. Mercy Ministries was becoming nationally known.

This widespread exposure caused an increase in the number of calls from troubled girls, but we had run out of room. It was heartbreaking to turn girls away because we lacked space. I knew we needed to expand the home so I began praying and seeking God for direction. While I was praying, God gave me a plan to step out in faith and expand the home; He also gave me the assurance that His ways are higher than our ways.

I met with the board to discuss the expansion. They were in favor of it but knew we did not have the money. I outlined the plan God had unfolded to me—we were to begin the building immediately, and that by the time the additions were completed, we would have the money to pay for it.

This was a major step of faith and some of the board members were concerned about approaching the project in this manner. They asked if I was *sure* this was what we were to do. I knew without a doubt that God wanted it done *exactly* as I described. After much discussion and prayer, we began building, trusting God to fulfill the plan He had outlined.

God worked through Jim and Kathy to help raise the support needed for the additions. The Lord had begun prospering their struggling business because of their obedience to tithing part of their profits back into God's work. They were also very involved with Mercy Ministries and knew we had taken the step of faith to expand the home.

They called to suggest a way to raise the money we needed. The Lord had recently blessed them with a sizeable contract, and they made a commitment to contribute ten thousand dollars to our project. They proposed a matching-funds program and challenged our advisory board and our contributors to a three-way matching-funds program. Every dollar given would mean a three dollar contribution!

The board accepted the challenge, making contributions and contacting friends to raise more money. The Edwards sent a direct mail letter to our contributors outlining the challenge.

We didn't raise thirty thousand dollars. God moved so mightily on people's hearts that we received forty-five thousand dollars, which paid for the entire expansion! We had taken the step of faith and God faithfully and mightily blessed us. The money we needed to pay for the final phase of construction came in just as the expansion was completed. We now had eight additional beds for girls, a large community bathroom area, a laundry room, a large classroom, and two more offices.

Once we finished the addition, we had an open house, which received television and newspaper coverage. Many of the people who received our direct mail attended, and we got to meet them for the first time. They saw firsthand what they had been contributing to and were very excited about what we were doing. This was the beginning of establishing relationships that have lasted for years.

Everyone at the open house was impressed (and some were a little surprised) with the home. The expansion was first class; we had even purchased new furniture. We took pride in our home and always trusted God to provide the best so the girls who came there would know they were loved. A run-down home and old, broken furniture would have communicated a different message. I had many opportunities to share with people how God had blessed us and provided for the expansion of the home.

What was even more amazing about our expansion was that it occurred at a time when Louisiana was one of the most economically depressed states in the country. The state was cutting back many of its welfare programs, and a group of community leaders was formed to find ways to make up for the decrease in available state aid. They asked us how Mercy Ministries could afford to expand while taxpayer-funded programs were being forced to shut down.

I explained to one of the women with the group that since we didn't receive government funds, we were not affected by the state's cutbacks.

"But people are going through a tough time as well," she responded, "so how are you able to raise *private* support?"

"The best way I know how to explain it," I said, "is that we operate according to kingdom principles. We believe God's Word is above natural circumstances. Even during hard economic times, His principles still work—they're not subject to what's going on in the natural realm. God said in the beginning of this ministry that if we would give at least ten percent of our income to other ministries and not charge the girls, He would always see that our needs were met. Because we've done that, despite the economic situation, God is still touching people to send us money.

"Even though times are tough, we have seen how God stands by His Word. For example, Luke 6:38 says, 'Give, and it shall be given to you; good measure, pressed down, and shaken together, and running over, shall men give into your bosom. For with the same measure that ye mete withal it shall be measured to you again' (KJV). Not only is He seeing that the needs of the ministry are being met by people giving to us. He is also meeting the needs of those who give to the ministry."

I was speaking rather boldly to this woman, but I felt a

responsibility to share with her exactly what we believed and make clear why we were able to prosper despite economic circumstances.

She was quiet for a few moments but finally smiled a little and said, "I was brought up in a Baptist church, and I can remember being taught about that when I was a kid. It's been a long time since I've thought about it, but I think I remember hearing that verse."

She seemed to be deep in thought as she left the home. To my surprise, not long after that visit she sent a contribution to us and continues to do so periodically.

I was thankful that God had provided Mercy Ministries with such a wonderful opportunity to tell about His faithfulness. He had taught me that, by following His Word, He would continue to use us, not only to help troubled girls, but to share the Gospel with others in the community. Experiences like that created in me a greater desire to remain faithful to God because I saw how He blessed obedience. By being part of Mercy Ministries, I was continually learning about how incredibly faithful God is to those who trust and obey Him.

God's Word says, "His lord said to him, 'Well done, good and faithful servant; you were faithful over a few things, I will make you ruler over many things. Enter into the joy of your lord'" (Matt. 25:21).

I was about to find out just how true that Scripture was.

4

By Divine Appointment
The Fulfillment of the Vision

For the vision is yet for an appointed time, but at the end it shall speak, and not lie: though it tarry, wait for it; because it will surely come, it will not tarry. (Habakkuk 2:3 KJV)

As we continued working with troubled girls I became increasingly concerned about responding to the tragedy of abortion. God had planted a seed within me several years earlier when I was leaving Teen Challenge to raise up His work in Monroe. He had given me a vision of a broader ministry that would include reaching out to unwed mothers, but He had not revealed the appointed time to expand the vision.

I knew from the Word that one thing God hates is "hands that shed innocent blood" (Proverbs 6:17). As I was reading my Bible one night, several verses stood out boldly:

> Rescue those who are unjustly sentenced to death; don't stand back and let them die. Don't try to disclaim responsibility by saying you didn't know about it. For God, who knows all hearts, knows yours, and he knows you knew! And he will reward everyone according to his deeds. (Proverbs 24:11-12 TLB)

When I thought of the pictures I had seen of the mangled and bloody bodies of aborted babies, this particular Scripture cut me to the heart with conviction. This is God's Word to His people, and it is up to us as Christians to effect a change! I vowed that night to share this verse in *every* church I spoke and to *every* group I met, to remind them of the millions of children whose lives are being taken prematurely each year by the unfortunate act of abortion.

That verse birthed in me the overwhelming desire to begin ministering to young girls who were pregnant outside the bonds of marriage. I prayed that God would provide the resources for an unwed mothers' home now that Mercy Ministries was firmly established and our expanded home was running smoothly.

The calls from unwed mothers had increased as the word had spread about how many troubled girls we were helping. Many of those who called were frightened and had no place to turn, and we desperately wanted to help them; but I didn't see how it was possible.

I expressed my regret to these young women, saying, "I'm sorry, we would like to help you but our home is not equipped to handle the special needs of expectant mothers. We hope to establish an unwed mothers' home someday, but until then..."

It was extremely difficult to turn these girls away because we sincerely wanted to help them. However, until God provided us the land and a building, I honestly felt like I had no other way to respond.

The Challenge

One morning while I was praying, God convicted me that my thinking was backward. I had expected God to provide us another home so we could accept unwed mothers. But God wanted us to step out in faith—first accept unwed mothers and then receive the home He would provide.

God showed me my hypocrisy in speaking out against abortion on the one hand and turning away pregnant girls on the other. His message was very clear—I was to stop talking against abortion unless I was ready to obey Him and begin taking in unwed mothers!

I felt a sense of relief, and asked Him to forgive me. I also promised Him that no matter what, I would never again turn away a pregnant girl He sent to us for help.

God wasted no time sending that girl! The very next day, we received a call from a thirteen-year-old who was pregnant by her mother's thirty-seven-year-old boyfriend. As I gripped the phone and listened to this helpless young girl cry out for help, the reality of the commitment I had made the day before came rushing over me. God was giving me another chance to do the right thing, and I was ready!

That was the beginning of one of the most rewarding decisions I have ever made.

It wasn't long before pregnant girls began calling us from all over the country. The more of them we took in the more fervent our prayers became for a new home. The needs were greater than our capacity to handle them in the present home.

As we prayed, believing God for the right direction, we began looking for property. Ideally, we would have preferred to add another, separate home next to the original home but there wasn't enough land left due to the expansions. We began looking for property nearby but couldn't find a suitable lot.

One day, a couple of the girls from the home went next door to take some fresh-baked banana nut bread to our neighbor, Mrs. Guidry. True to our word, we had befriended the elderly mother of the man who sold us his home. She was in her mid-eighties and needed someone to check on her periodically. We frequently took her cookies and other home-baked goodies and enjoyed visiting with her. When the girls came back, they told me Mrs. Guidry wanted to see me.

I finished a couple of things at the office and walked the few steps to her house. I knocked on the door and Mrs. Guidry greeted me with her warm smile and invited me inside. She was a precious Catholic lady who was very committed to God. We had all grown to love her. Although it was always good to see her, today she appeared a little worn and tired. Nevertheless, she was in good spirits and asked me to sit down.

"Mrs. Guidry," I said, "the girls told me you wanted to see me. Is everything okay?"

"Yes, everything is fine although I haven't been feeling very well lately. I guess that's to be expected when you get to be my age. In fact, that's part of what I wanted to talk to you about.

"I've been so tired and I've really been talking to the Lord, and I believe that He's shown me than I'm not going to be here much longer." She smiled as she continued. "But I'm ready to go and I'm trying to settle all my affairs. I've been thinking about what I want to do with my property. I know your ministry has grown a lot and that you don't have much room to expand. I was wondering if you might be interested in having my property after I'm gone?"

"Yes, Mrs. Guidry, I would be interested." I spoke softly, trying to be sensitive to her feelings.

"Well, I'd love to be able to give it to you, but I'm not in a position to do that. I don't want my family to have to be responsible for my funeral and other expenses once I'm gone. But I would like for you to have the first option to buy my property. I'll tell my son we've talked, and ask him to make sure he sells it to you at a fair price.

"Now, if you were to buy this property, what would you do with it?" she asked me.

"Mrs. Guidry, we really need more property to build an unwed mothers' home. Right now we have more girls calling us than we're able to help. If we bought your property, we would probably have your house moved and build a home for unwed mothers here. That way girls in trouble would have a place to come instead of going to abortion clinics."

Tears came to her eyes as she looked at me and said, "Nancy, I can't think of anything I'd like better than to know that my property would be used for that."

I was touched by Mrs. Guidry's desire to help us. I told her how much she meant to us and what a blessing it was that she wanted us to have her property. I prayed with her before I left that day and asked God to bless her and keep His hand on her and I thanked Him for her.

About three months later Mrs. Guidry went on to be with the Lord. At her funeral I thought about what a wonderful neighbor and friend she had been. We would all miss her. I also thought about her desire to help us grow, and I was filled with gratitude that God had put her in our lives.

Mrs. Guidry's son, Lawrence, called me a couple of days after the funeral and asked if we would like to buy her property. I assured him we did, and he gave us a reasonable price.

It was obvious that God had opened this door to us, and the advisory board agreed that we should purchase the property. We all shared the vision of expanding Mercy Ministries to reach out to unwed mothers, and the property included more than enough land to build the home. Within a short time we had enough money to make a down payment. Once we sold the house and had it moved, we paid the balance and owned the land debt free.

Now that we had the land we were faced with the challenge of finding a way to raise the money to build. We took a picture of a pregnant girl sitting on the vacant lot and placed it on the refrigerator door as a reminder to the staff and girls to pray, believing for our new maternity home. We thanked Him in advance for making a way for us.

We sent out a newsletter informing our supporters of our need. While many of them gave generously, we did not have nearly enough money to start construction. Although it seemed in the natural realm that raising the money we needed was impossible, we knew God had a plan. We just weren't sure what it was.

Resisting Temptations

One morning while I was working in my office I received a call.

"Hello," said a man's voice, "my wife and I have heard about your work and we think it's wonderful."

"Thank you," I responded.

"We've been told that part of your ministry includes taking in unwed mothers and that you are trying to build a new home for them."

"Yes, sir."

"I am quite wealthy and could easily supply you with sufficient funding to establish the home you want to build. Is it true that you need some financial help?"

I sat up expectantly. "We sure do," I answered.

"Well, to get to the point, my wife and I are very much interested in adopting a baby, and if you were to supply us with one, you could name the amount you need."

I paused for a moment, shocked by what I had just heard. Finally I said, "Sir, if you want to adopt, I'll send you an application form, but there's no need for you to give us a penny. We seek God's direction and guidance in the placement of each child. If you want to send a contribution, that would be wonderful, but it will in no way increase your chances of adopting a child from us."

"You mean to tell me we can't get some preferential treatment in exchange for building your new home?" he asked angrily. "How do you expect to build it?"

"I don't know," I said, trying not to sound upset. "But I do know that if we ever accepted money for a baby, God would remove His blessing from this ministry so fast we wouldn't last another month!"

That's how I turned down the opportunity to start a career in baby selling. That was not the only temptation I had to resist during the time we were waiting on the Lord to supply us with the means to build the home. Another morning I received an unexpected phone call from the governor's office.

"Miss Alcorn, I'm from the office of Governor Buddy Roemer. We'd like you to know that the outstanding work you've been doing through Mercy Ministries with troubled girls has come to our attention. We are very impressed with what we've heard."

I was pleasantly surprised. I knew our work had received some public attention, but I had no idea that news of what we were doing had traveled to the state capital. This was even more evidence that God was granting us favor.

"Well, that's not the only reason I called. We understand that you want to build a second home for unwed mothers."

"That's right," I replied. "We have property next door, but right now I have no idea where we're going to get the money to build. So far, the funding just hasn't come in."

"I'm calling to talk about the possibility of state funding for your home. We would like to help you because we know there's a tremendous need for this type of facility. Given the reputation of Mercy Ministries, we think this would be a worthy cause for the State of Louisiana to support."

I caught my breath. We had a backlog of unwed mothers who needed our help. The sooner the home was built, the better. By all appearances, I was being offered a way to have the home built immediately. But appearances can be deceiving.

"Well, thank you very much for the offer. I'm so pleased that your office thinks well enough of Mercy Ministries to want to provide support. And it's true, we need a sizeable amount of money to build our home." I continued, "But if we were to start taking state aid, it could jeopardize the heart of what we are trying to do. We're a Christ-centered ministry, which is the very thing that makes us successful in working with the girls. If someone ever challenged that in court, we would probably have to take the Christian content out of our program simply because we were receiving government funds. It would be like prayer in school—someone would call it a violation of the separation of church and state."

There was a pause at the other end of the line as she thought about what I said. "You know, you're probably right."

I thanked her for the governor's interest in Mercy Ministries and told her it was flattering. I wanted to make sure she wasn't offended by my refusal of her offer. She assured me she respected my position, and we ended the call on good terms.

When I hung up, we still had a piece of property with no home on it; we still had pregnant girls staying in a home designed for girls with other types of problems; and there were still many girls we were unable to help because we had no room for them.

I knew God would provide for the needs of Mercy Ministries, just as He had in the past, but I didn't know how or when. I did know that I had just turned down a sizeable amount of money.

If I had not spent eight years working for the state government, I might not have been able to resist the temptation of their aid. Because I had seen all that the government had to offer, I knew that any help we provided to troubled girls and unwed mothers had to be free of government support. Without the freedom to teach God's Word and allow Him to transform lives, we would become just another empty social program with no hope to give the girls.

I told the girls and staff about the offers I had received. "We are not going to compromise," I said emphatically, as much for my own benefit as theirs. "God has a plan for how He's going to raise up this home and it will be in His perfect timing. The devil has tried to get us to compromise our convictions to get it built sooner, but we're not going to succumb to the wiles of the devil. We will continue to pray and stand on God's Word and believe."

The Reward

Two months after posting our "faith picture" on the refrigerator, and right on the heels of the two offers for financial aid, I was invited to speak at a week-long evangelistic conference in Las Vegas. The meeting was wonderful, but by the time it was over I was exhausted. As I slipped into my plane seat, I closed my eyes and hoped no one would sit next to me.

"Excuse me."

I opened my eyes to see a medium-sized man standing over me wearing blue jeans, a T-shirt, and tennis shoes. I moved to let him squeeze by and hoped he wouldn't start talking to me. I was so tired all I wanted was to take a nap.

God had other plans. Even before he fastened his seat belt, he turned to me and asked, "So how much money did you lose gambling in Las Vegas this week?"

I sat up almost regretfully. When someone asks me a question like that, I feel obligated to share what I believe.

"I didn't come here to gamble," I said. "I don't do that."

He looked at me quizzically and said, "I've never heard of someone coming to Las Vegas and not gambling. What else is there to do?"

I spent the next two-and-a-half hours describing my work and answering his questions. When we landed in Dallas-Fort Worth, he asked, "Nancy, do you have a brochure about what you do? I'd like to have one."

I pulled one out of my carry-on and handed it to him as I headed toward my connecting flight. Since Mercy Ministries was so much a part of my life, I frequently talked with people about it and many times gave them our literature. Once we parted, I didn't give our meeting much thought.

Four weeks later I got a long-distance phone call. "Nancy, I don't know if you remember me or not. I'm the man who sat next to you on the flight from Las Vegas."

"Sure I remember. I gave you one of our brochures. Have you been back to Las Vegas?"

"No, I haven't, and that's part of what I'm calling about. Your story prompted so much thought in me the past few weeks that I haven't been able to get Mercy Ministries off my mind. I had so many things I wanted to tell you that day on the plane, but we ran out of time. I don't think I even told you my name."

He went on, "I became a Christian just three months before I met you. In the past, whenever I was under pressure, I would go to Las Vegas and gamble. This last time it all felt so empty that I decided to go home, but when I got ready to leave, it was like there was almost a physical force holding me there. I couldn't figure it out at the time but have finally come to the conclusion that I was supposed to be on that flight to meet you. I'm not used to this 'being led by God' stuff yet, but every time I pray I keep feeling like there is something I'm supposed to help you build. Are you trying to build something?"

"Yes, we already have land to build an unwed mothers' home."

He was silent for a moment, and when he began to speak again, he was crying. "Forty years ago," he told me, "I was born to a teenage girl who had been raped. I never met my birth mother, but I'm sure, considering the circumstances, that if there hadn't been a place for her to go, I would have been aborted.

"I was adopted when I was five days old and have always been very close to my adoptive mother. Last year she died and left me several million dollars. Ever since her death, I've been looking for something special I could do in her memory that I thought would be pleasing to her. How much more money do you need?"

I took a deep breath and said, "A hundred and fifty thousand dollars."

"You've got it."

I was absolutely stunned. I couldn't believe what I was hearing. When I regained my composure, I shared with him all the events that had led up to this point. I told him how God had dealt with me to be willing to take in unwed mothers despite the fact that we weren't really equipped to handle their needs. I described how we'd acquired the land and about our faith picture and how the need was so great that we had been praying and believing for God to provide a way to build the home.

Although there were no strings attached to his generous gift, he did make one stipulation. He said it would be okay to tell the story of how the home was built but asked that I never reveal his name.

When I got off the phone I let out a yell. One of my staff rushed into my office to see what was wrong.

I was so overjoyed I could hardly speak. "We've got it! We've got it! We've got it!" I was almost dancing around the room.

"Got what?"

"Our new home! The rest of our new home is paid for!"

When the staff realized what I was talking about, we were all literally jumping up and down with joy. The girls had joined us by then and were ecstatic. We phoned all the members of our advisory board immediately to share the good news and even placed a few long-distance calls to some of our supporters to let them know how God had so richly blessed us. We were so excited that we could finally build the home.

The Unwed Mothers' Home

Mercy Ministries held a ground-breaking ceremony for the unwed mothers' home, followed by an open house in our existing home. It was a time of food and fellowship to which we invited civic and community leaders as well as our board members and supporters. Two television crews were present to broadcast the occasion on the local evening news, and a large group of onlookers gathered.

Best of all, the mayor of West Monroe was present to witness the event and participate in the ground-breaking ceremony. "I never thought there would even be one home—much less two," he stated in front of television cameras. "But this is a perfect example of what can happen when we put our faith and trust in God."

It is always a joy when God uses Mercy Ministries not only to bring restoration to the broken lives of the troubled girls and unwed mothers who come to us for help, but also to be an example to the world of the reality of Jesus Christ. By remaining faithful to the way God wanted things done, Mercy Ministries provided the mayor an opportunity to publicly bear witness to the power of God.

It was incredible to see the home go up little by little and know that it had already been paid for. Every morning when I looked out at the construction I thought back to our obedience to God by opening our doors to unwed mothers, starting with that thirteen-year-old girl, and how God had once again rewarded us for our step of faith and belief in His provision.

When the maternity home was almost finished, "the man on the plane" came to Monroe to see what he was helping to build. He didn't want to go inside, but simply asked me to pull up in front of the home. He got out of the car and stood there looking at it for a long time. When he turned to face me there were tears rolling down his face.

"You know, Nancy, when I think of all the girls who are going to come to this home from all over the country to give their babies a chance, it seems like such a small amount of money for the difference it's going to make in the lives of so many people. I'm excited about what you're doing here, and I know it would make my mother very happy."

To this day, this precious man still calls every few months to see how things are going. He has since married, and he and his wife have become personal friends of mine.

In order to furnish the home, I spoke at churches and civic groups, challenging them with the story of the man on the plane. "God is going to continue to meet our needs just like

He has in the past and just as He promises in His Word," I would tell them. "If God has laid it on your heart to be used by Him to help us, we will be very grateful. But before you decide whether you want to give, I would like for you to think about something: how many of you would put old, used furniture in a brand-new house you just built? If you would, please raise your hand."

No one in the audience ever raised their hand. "Then you'll understand that we feel the same way. A new home needs new furniture, not old furniture you're about to get rid of.

"The Lord has dealt with me that not only should we tell these girls that Jesus loves them, we should also set an example that God wants them to have His best. That starts with our willingness to expect the best. We can't expect these girls to regain their sense of self-worth if they come to a home that's filled with old, worn-out furniture. A local furniture store has already committed to selling us new furniture at cost, and your gifts will be used accordingly."

Many people had advised me to try to raise funds by projecting poverty. Their contention was that, if I told people Mercy Ministries was in desperate need we could get more contributions. I never believed we should talk to people like that because it doesn't demonstrate faith in God. If we stand up and proclaim poverty, that's what we'll receive.

Instead, when I speak at fund-raising events I proclaim that God is Jehovah Jireh, our provider. He provides not only for Mercy Ministries, but also for those who give. People have consistently responded to these appeals because they appreciate the fact that I don't try to manipulate them.

When the construction was completed, we had an official dedication that was covered by all the newspapers and television news crews. Once again, they reported on the incredible way we were provided the funds and the furniture. We were proud of our new home, and it was rewarding to have the local media inform the community with such a strong testimony of God's power.

Not only did God provide us with a new, furnished home that was entirely paid for, but we were also given a new van about the time the home opened. A local insurance agent provided insurance for the van free of charge.

With the opening of the unwed mothers' home, a steady stream of girls began flowing in. All types of girls came to us. They ranged in age from 13 to 30, but the average age was about 16. Their backgrounds varied. Some came from broken homes, some from Christian homes. A few had been taken advantage of, others had simply made a mistake. Some had family support, many had no support and nowhere to turn. Regardless of the circumstances that brought them to us, we took them in and taught them about God's love and forgiveness and supported their decisions to have their babies.

Our program centers around the needs and personal growth of each girl as an individual. She has made the decision to have her baby, and we pray with her and support her throughout her pregnancy right through labor and delivery.

It's always exciting around the home when it's time for one of the girls to go to the hospital to have her baby. I'll never forget the first time I saw a baby being born. When we started taking in unwed mothers, one of the first girls to come to the home asked me to go into delivery with her.

Words hardly describe the feelings I had when I witnessed the beauty and miracle of a new life, a brand-new baby, making its way into this world. I was enveloped by a sense of God's love and His incredible power to create life. In the moment I first saw that newborn baby, God spoke to my heart that this was the first of many, many babies to come that would be saved from abortion and allowed to live because of Mercy Ministries. I was overwhelmed with the knowledge that countless numbers of people in the future would be affected because of God's love and provision for these girls. I was speechless.

When a girl comes to our home, she is given the choice of

keeping her baby or giving it up for adoption. If the girl chooses adoption, we allow her to sit down with us and describe what she wants in an adoptive couple. We believe God gives these girls the desire of their hearts, and whatever the desire, He'll work through it to bring the couple that He has chosen to raise that particular child. It's incredible how God sees to it that it's a perfect match.

In a different way, it was equally exciting the first time I walked in and handed a three-day-old baby to its new parents. The first couple who adopted from us had been asking God for years to give them a family. When they held that baby for the first time we laughed and we cried tears of joy. Their hearts were filled with gratitude for God and for the young girl who had given them the most precious gift anyone could ever give.

Over the years I have witnessed many births and we have presented many babies to adoptive couples. The joy and excitement we experience is as dramatic and lasting as the first time. It never gets old—never!

When these girls choose life over abortion, they may well be making the biggest decision of their life. Many who have been to Mercy Ministries have had one or more abortions in the past because they had nowhere to turn. One thing we do is to pray with them to receive God's forgiveness and ask Him to cleanse them of their guilt and remorse. We also train them in the ways of God as we do the girls in the other home, so when they leave they will be prepared to live in obedience to God's Word and to fulfill what He has for them to do.

As Christians, it is not enough to simply ask a girl *not* to have an abortion. We must provide an alternative and teach her the truth. We must not condemn, but rather *reach out* to these confused and misguided girls. Otherwise, we leave them little choice. We cannot disclaim responsibility. We cannot stand by and let babies die. We are to be a lifeline.

The seed that had been planted long before had come to

fruition. God had fulfilled His promise and poured His blessing on Mercy Ministries. The lives of many were being saved, restored, and fulfilled. And this was just the beginning!

5

The Transformation
Process

An Inside Look

And be not conformed to this world: but be ye transformed by the renewing of your mind, that ye may prove what is that good, and acceptable, and perfect, will of God. (Romans 12:2 KJV)

He was probably the cutest dog I had ever seen. Because I felt he would provide an even better home environment for the girls, I purchased Malachi from a breeder of national champion shelties. The breeder later told me, "You pray for good homes for your babies and I pray for good homes for mine."

We had enjoyed Malachi for three years when one day there was a knock on the door. One of the girls opened the door to see a neighbor with a look of anxious concern on her face. "There's a dog in the street that just got hit by a car. I'm afraid it's yours."

Thinking Malachi was playing in the backyard, one of the girls ran to check, only to find him gone.

I was gone at the time, but I later learned that the staff on duty and a couple girls ran to the street, where Malachi was barely alive. They rushed him to the vet, but he could not be saved.

I came home about the time they returned from the vet. My heart was broken when I was told what had happened. We buried Malachi on the property.

Though he was only an animal, we had all developed a special bond with him. Malachi had been the "family" pet. His death to us was like a member of our family dying.

Many of the girls had come to Mercy Ministries hardened from past hurts, and for them, this small dog was the first creature they had felt real affection for.

As I dealt with my own grief, I wrote to the breeder who sold us Malachi. I wasn't sure I was ready for another dog. I just wanted him to know what had happened. Shortly after writing I broke down and called him. "I was waiting for your call," he said. "I just had a litter and the runt is the only one left. He is six weeks old and really cute. The Lord told me I was to give him to you. I'll fly him out this Monday."

As I waited for Monday to arrive I prayed for God to give me a name for our new puppy. The name Nehemiah kept invading my thoughts. "What does that name mean?" I wondered. I looked it up and found it meant "comforter." I thought the Lord meant He would bring us comfort over the loss of Malachi. Little did I know that over the next few years he would bring comfort to hundreds of girls who have called Mercy Ministries home.

When a girl was sick, Nehemiah would sit by her side. When one was confined to her bed because of a danger she'll miscarry, Nehemiah would be right there beside her. If there were twenty girls in a room and one was emotionally hurting, Nehemiah would go straight to her. He truly had a gift for comforting. The death of Malachi and the arrival of Nehemiah allowed the girls to see God's love and provision in the little things of life. Satan caused us grief by stealing the life of our dog, but the girls were able to see how God restores and that He cares about everything that touches our lives, even the smallest detail.

Why Mercy Ministries

Many times I have been asked, "Why do you want to build special homes for these girls? Why not simply let them live with Christian families where they will be exposed to the Gospel in a *real* home?"

The problem with this idea is that in this day and age parents have enough difficulty bringing up their own children in the ways of the Lord. How much more difficult it is to invest the time to give direction to a girl going through immense spiritual and emotional turmoil. They would be unable to provide a girl the around-the-clock, intense, personal discipleship she needs. They would also place their own children at risk by subjecting them to the influence of these girls which is often anything but Christ-like. Unless God has divinely called a family to take such risks for the sake of a troubled girl or unwed mother, it will not prosper as God would intend. Usually, the girl leaves her mark on the family instead of the family leaving Christ's mark on her.

In addition, these girls need constant care; and a family cannot give that much time because of all the other commitments they have. Furthermore, the girls need to be in a structured program where they will be taught, counseled and prayed for according to the Word of God.

Mercy Ministries serves as a type of intensive care unit for these spiritually wounded girls. We do our best to provide the girls not with a facility but with a home. We try to make every detail of their environment as domestic as possible, down to having a dog for the girls to love. The place these girls stay should provide all the privileges and responsibilities of belonging to a family. It should not have an institutional atmosphere, but should encourage personal relationships and harmonious growth.

This is especially important for girls who have never experienced a stable, healthy home environment, one where they are affectionately nurtured in Christian love and taught biblical values. Many of them have spent their lives in rebellion against their family's values and need a second chance to learn those values that they once rebelled against. These girls, whether raised in Christian or non-Christian homes, need to know that Christ-like love is not judgmental but gentle, gracious, and merciful.

A Day in the Lives of Our Girls

The girls get up at seven each weekday morning. While requiring a time for them to get up may seem insignificant, it lays a foundation of discipline upon which they can build things of greater value in the future.

The process of training these young women to live with some kind of routine is not always easy; some have never known routine or responsibility. Between seven and nine, they eat breakfast. Each girl then has specific duties she has been asked to be responsible for. If they are made to feel that their contribution is significant to the other family members, they can develop a sense of self-esteem and pride in their work. Some fix breakfast, some clean up afterward, and others help around the house. Everyone's interaction makes Mercy Ministries feel like home and causes them to be proud of their part in keeping their home inviting.

The girls are taught that since they receive so much during their stay at the home they should give of themselves in return. We expect no more than what they would do if it were their own homes. These small chores are extremely important in improving the girls' self-confidence and teaching them responsibility. We teach the staff to continually praise them when they have given of themselves to others at the home. For many of the girls this is the first time they have been given a job and offered praise for doing it well. If they complain about having to do these tasks, we usually give them more work to do until they learn to do their part willingly.

Soon after we began taking in girls, we realized that

although we were telling them to spend time in God's Word each day, we needed to give them an opportunity to have a regularly scheduled quiet time so everyone could benefit. Each morning we have a time set aside for daily devotions, and we start each new girl on a specific Bible reading program. While most of the girls do not stay at the home for a full year, we hope we impart to them a daily habit that will carry over after they leave the home.

During the day we also try to show the girls the importance of corporate praise and worship. By worshiping together, the girls become closer both to God and to one another and hopefully realize the need to be in fellowship with other Christian believers. Had it not been for the Christian friends I had praying for me, there are many times I don't know if I would have made it.

Bible classes are also a positive part of the girls' time here. During this time we will invite a guest speaker to minister to them, use a video, or one of the staff will teach and share practical application through her own experiences. Discussion is an important element of this, and we always give the girls an opportunity to express how they feel about what has been taught. I never throw out information without giving them a chance to respond. If we are talking about hurts and they are hurting, we want to introduce them to the God who heals. If they are struggling with sin, they need to know about the power of the Holy Spirit that enables them to be victorious. If they are oppressed, they need to know that Jesus freed them from oppression. We give the girls every opportunity to ask questions and hopefully receive revelation about what they do not understand. We also give them opportunities to be prayed for individually as they feel the need.

But what would life be like without free time? Everyone needs time for rest and relaxation. The girls have daily opportunities for recreation as well as special activities from time to time. Our library is filled with Christian books, teaching tapes, and Christian music, which we encourage the girls to use. If the weather is nice, the girls will often sit outside and read their Bibles or Christian books, or simply enjoy spending time with one another.

Once a week each of the girls meets with a counselor. At these sessions, each girl is prayed with and given counsel to help her through personal struggles. A counselor will often ask a girl to write an essay on what the Bible says about an issue she is facing. For example, if a girl is struggling with being unable to forgive her mother, the counselor might ask her to look up Scriptures that deal with forgiveness and write about how she could apply what they say to her own life. In writing what is in their hearts, they are often able to see more clearly what areas of their life need divine intervention. The girls are encouraged to be painfully honest in what they write. If a girl realizes she needs to forgive her mother, for example, but does not feel that she is able, she is encouraged to say so. Her honesty gives the counselor a chance to deal with the real problem and provide a real solution. Forgiveness is a decision, not an emotion. If a girl waits for a feeling, she will never truly forgive anyone. Through the counseling process the things that truly held her in chains have been broken by the time a girl leaves the home. And by the never-failing and unchanging power of God she has been set free.

In dealing with girls from all walks of life I have realized that some have never learned to enjoy some of the simple pleasures of being a woman. Therefore, along with our basic Bible and Christian living classes, we offer classes on basic living skills. For example, volunteers give classes on cooking, budgeting, skills necessary for job interviewing and filling out job applications, etiquette, proper dress, cosmetics, and overall improvement of appearance. We also offer General Equivalency Diploma classes to those who need them. A "virtuous woman" as spoken of in Proverbs 31, is one who truly represents Christ. We teach the girls that they should work to become the best in every area of life. We encourage them that there is nothing wrong with making the most of their appearance or dressing nicely or having a challenging career. When people look at the children of God they should see the best the kingdom has to offer. We try to make these girls the most productive and well-rounded individuals they can be by the time they leave our care and reenter a progressive society.

After evening classes the girls have more free time. Quiet time begins at ten, giving them time to wind down, and lights out at ten-thirty. I firmly believe this is one of the most productive times in their day. They can sit and digest and analyze what has been made available to them during their day. And they can seek the Lord for clear understanding. A staff member prays with the girls at bedtime, asking the Lord to guard their minds that they may rest. This is vital as many of the girls are subject to nightmares due to the detestable events and traumas they have endured. We assure the girls that if they are awakened by bad dreams they may come to the staff member on duty that night and she will pray with them. We hope that each girl will eventually come to be strong enough in her faith in the Lord's ability to guard her mind that she will pray for herself and claim God's promise in Psalm 127:2—that "He gives His beloved sleep."

One of the ways we are able to maintain such a warm Christian environment in the homes is through our intake procedures. All the girls who come to Mercy Ministries come of their own choosing. They can't be sent to the homes by their parents or anyone else. Before they apply, we send them an application form that lists all the rules they must follow. This filters out those who do not have a true desire to be helped or who are unwilling to submit to authority. The ones who do come have a fiber somewhere in the depths of their soul that longs to be released from this world of bondage. To verify their seriousness in seeking help we also conduct an intake interview.

While we have been criticized for the way we filter the girls who come to us, without our stringent screening process we could not create a family environment in our homes. If we were to accept girls who are not serious about their lives being restored, they would be stumbling blocks to those who are. We are incapable of helping young women who are not willing to be helped. Until they choose to cooperate with the methods we feel the Lord has directed us to use, there is nothing we can do but pray for them.

Through a close, home-like environment God uses the girls to build character in each other. Most of them are used to doing their own thing and looking out for themselves. In the some-times painful testing process of dealing with a house full of women, the girls are forced to learn to treat other people as Christ would, forgiving as well as asking for forgiveness. We often refer to the girls as "sandpaper sisters," keeping in mind that as "iron sharpens iron, so a man sharpens the countenance of his friend" (Proverbs 27:17).

We assure the girls that if they will not give up on each other—despite their fights and arguments—they will even-tually see the fruit of their labor in their ability to be open with others and to trust, two important skills that have been suppressed because of the destructive life-styles they have lived. "You're diamonds in the rough," we tell them, "and God is using you to polish one another and smooth over the rough edges." Our goal for them is that each will gain a per-sonal realization of her position in Christ, that she stands righteous before God and has full authority as a believer, which allows her to claim victory over any circumstances she might face. In Luke 10:19, Jesus tells His disciples, "Behold, I give unto you power to tread on serpents and scorpions, and over all the power of the enemy: and nothing shall by any means hurt you" (KJV).

In addition to individual counseling sessions, once a week

the girls gather for a group session led by a staff counselor. The counselor encourages the girls to be open with one another and to tear down walls built by years of pain. For example the counselor might say, "Tonight, I want to go around the room and have each of you share one of your strengths and one of your weaknesses." As they discover where their weaknesses and strengths lie they begin to see the qualities they may lack that someone else has, and the qualities they have may be essential to aiding someone else's growth in Christ. That is why we are one body with many members—so that our strengths can complement each other. Now that we know each other's strengths and weaknesses, we can pray for one another effectively. In this way we teach the girls to trust and share with one another, so they are prepared for their future relationships and their future ministries.

The Medical Model

"Hello, Nancy. My wife and I need your help again." The voice over the phone sounded weary and distressed. This couple had called several weeks earlier to ask my advice about their legal rights with their daughter's doctor. The doctor had decided that, since their daughter had turned thirteen, she ought to prescribe birth control pills for her because she would soon be sexually active. The couple explained to the doctor that they did not want their daughter to have the pills because they were raising her to live as a Christian, but the doctor ignored the parents' request and gave them to her secretly.

"What seems to be the problem?" I asked, trying to sound reassuring. Since beginning the first home, I have often received calls from parents asking for counsel.

"We're having more problems with our daughter." The voice paused. "She sneaked out of the house in the middle of the night. We caught her smoking and drinking with her friends. As far as we know this is the first time she has done this. She told us she just wanted to see what it was like. All her friends are trying it. We felt compelled to get help for her, so we took her to a counselor."

"What did the counselor say?" I asked.

"Well, that's what surprised us. The counselor said she probably has serious problems and that we should commit her to a treatment program where she can be kept on medication and locked up for observation for a month. Somehow that seems a little too radical to my wife and me. What do you think?"

"I think the Lord's given you great wisdom. You can't medicate a spirit of rebellion."

Mercy Ministries has received many girls from troubled homes who have been through at least one secular treatment center—some have been to as many as ten. Some of the girls who come to us with drug addiction problems were put on prescription drugs by doctors to help them overcome their addiction to illegal drugs. Others have used medication as a way to cover up the effects of sin, which needs repentance and forgiveness, not drugs. In my experience, this kind of treatment only masks the problems temporarily. How can people who have no heart knowledge of Christ and His delivering power solve a problem that goes beyond the realm of medical diagnosis? These psychiatric treatment centers bleed insurance companies out of thousands of dollars a day, and when the insurance runs out, the patient is sent home. In many cases it is nothing more than a money-making industry. These girls do not need big medical terminology, expensive medication, and treatment programs to cure their ills—they need to see clearly that sin is the problem and that they can have new life in Christ.

In contrast to the ways of the world. Mercy Ministries makes things very clear. Each girl is held accountable for her own actions whether they lead to her success or her demise. No matter how good she is or how bad, only through confessing her sin and believing in Jesus Christ can she taste true forgiveness. With this simple message, God has used Mercy Ministries to bring restoration to broken lives time and time again.

Young women have come to Mercy Ministries so tattered and torn that even I am skeptical. "Okay, Lord," I often think, "I can't wait to see how You are going to pull this one off." They are enslaved to sin and burdened with guilt and shame from the past. I love to sit back and watch God perform a total transformation. Instead of changing only the surface of their lives, the Word of God reaches into those secret places of their hearts and divides between soul and spirit, discerning the very thoughts and intents of the heart (see Heb. 4:12).

Choosing Between Life and Death

The Gospel does not guarantee that every young woman who comes to us will automatically be restored. One of the major ways a Christian ministry differs from a secular treatment program is that a Christian knows that people can, and often do, reject mercy. We do everything humanly possible to save girls from self-destruction, but we cannot make their choices. And God does not make them either. For He said in His Word, "I have set before you life and death, blessings and curses. Now choose life, so that you and your children may live and that you may love the LORD your God, listen to his voice, and hold fast to him" (Deuteronomy 30:19-20 NIV).

The only way I can explain the painful agony some girls endure and the ultimate deception of the enemy is to paint a picture of a graphic, but heartbreakingly true story. Rachel came to us after she had experienced remarkably horrible treatment at the hands of almost every person she should have been able to trust. The following paragraphs are an actual account of some of the gruesome events of Rachel's life as told to her counselor in one-on-one sessions. Of course, the names have been changed.

First Counseling Session 6/7/90

- Rachel has suffered physical, mental, and sexual abuse. Before she was five or six years old, she had been sexually abused by several of her mother's boyfriends. Rachel's mother was promiscous; she had a mixed baby, whom she beat to death when she was drunk. Rachel's mother showed no remorse. The police covered it up because they slept with her mom. Rachel's mom told her about this and that she did not feel bad. Later, Rachel used drugs and did the same things her mom had done. Rachel feels she has now forgiven her mother. Her mom does not want Rachel. Rachel does not know if her father was her real dad. Around five or six years of age Rachel was taken away from her mother. She stayed with an elderly woman who was a Christian and they went to church. When she was twelve years old she asked Jesus to come into her heart.
- Then Rachel was adopted by non-Christians—John and Patty Sanders. John abused her sexually as well as physically and mentally. Patty told her daughters she didn't love them or want them. John had intercourse with Rachel several times. He abused her and played with her mind; threatened her, and told her not to tell anyone he had sex with her.
- Her second foster parents were wealthy. They did not abuse her, but she became suicidal because of her past.
- Rachel next lived in a group home. There was no abuse. She graduated. She loved school and lived at the group home for two years. During this time, Rachel read horoscopes and a counselor predicted her future with tarot cards.

Counseling Session 6/20/90

- Rachel has low self-esteem. She gets angry at herself because she is not perfect. Rachel's mom used to beat her up when she was small. Once she was beaten with a plank that had nails in it. Rachel's mom would tell her, "You can't do anything right." Rachel's adoptive mother, Patty Sanders, beat her and her sister Jennifer. She would leave welts and bruises on them. Patty accused both of them of taking away her husband. Tim Jordan, another foster parent, hit Rachel in the face because he was angry at her for not being able to drive a stick-shift truck.

- When Rachel lived with Ms. Baker, an elderly Christian woman, Rachel started beating herself. She wanted to please Ms. Baker. She used to beat herself up, ending up with a black eye and a bloody nose. She would completely lose control.

- Rachel's mom didn't name her. When she was born a nurse gave her a name. When Rachel was adopted by the Sanders, they gave her the name Rachel. Rachel was angry at her mom for not naming her.

- Rachel's brother Greg used to beat her up. He was five years older than she. Mitch and Greg, her brothers, repeatedly raped and sexually abused her. Wendell, another brother, was good; he never touched her.

Counseling Session 6/27/90

- Tyrone, the father of Rachel's baby, sells drugs and is a pimp. Rachel had sexual relations with Tyrone (who was manipulative and controlling), Mike Daniels, Dwayne, Kevin (miscarried his baby), George, Don Farmer, and Leroy (he's dead now; was shot in the head over money).

Counseling Session 7/24/90

- Rachel had a counselor, Tina Bellows. Tina said she did not understand how Rachel would make it. She thought Rachel should be put in an institution.

Counseling Session 8/14/90

- Some of her neighbors said that while Rachel's mom worked at a beer joint, she left the kids in the car. The children would get out and play in a nearby dumpster. The neighbors also said they saw them eating out of the dump. Rachel now has a problem with her weight. She's afraid she won't have any food to eat, like in the past. Her adoptive parents told her she was obese. They would make her run three miles and she had to weigh in every day. She would sneak food. Rachel didn't understand why men abused her. She told herself she was going to get fatter so men wouldn't look at her. But Rachel also hated herself because she couldn't lose weight. She would beat herself for it. Ms. Baker never disciplined her harshly.

- Rachel's mom had killed one of Rachel's brothers so Rachel vowed she'd never have children because she didn't want to treat them the way her mom treated her. Rachel has had two miscarriages. She told Tyrone their baby that she was expecting was a mistake. Tyrone told her he hoped she got AIDS and died.

Counseling Session 8/28/90

- Rachel said she had vowed that if she ever had a baby girl she would not let her husband ever touch her or even be close to her. Rachel also vowed that if she ever married and her husband beat her or her kids, she would kill him. Rachel fears death, spanking children, and being beaten. She remembers times when she was young: she would try to run away, she lived in the woods, she would run and run and run. Scooter, her mom's boyfriend, would chase her and beat her and torment her. He would burn her with cigarettes and beat her with a two-by-four. He would poke her and say he was going to beat her. Scooter sexually abused her. Then her mom would hit her repeatedly.

Counseling Session 10/17/90

- Rachel told us about a letter from her mom. Her mother

turned her life over to God after reading Rachel's letter. She has given up smoking and drinking. Her mom has cancer, diabetes, arthritis, heart problems, and many other things wrong with her. Rachel wants to see her sometime, but wants to be ready.

Counseling Session 11/7/90

- When she was six years old, Rachel drowned a puppy. Her mom and a friend had fought and taken it out on the kids. Rachel was angry with her mom so took it out on the puppy. She put her puppy under the water and made him stay under there. She didn't want him to get out. It was an accident.
- Rachel watched the movie *Benji*; and this upset her. It reminded her of the time Scooter, her mom's boyfriend, had tortured her and her brothers and her dogs in the front yard. Rachel was about three or four years old. He killed her dogs in front of her—he took the only thing she had. Rachel wanted Scooter dead. She begged a man named Tony to kill him. Scooter abused her brothers and she hated him for it. Scooter made her do back bends without her clothes on for one hour. He forced her to perform perverse acts against her will. He locked her out of the house while he abused her brothers, but she could hear them screaming.

Counseling Session 11/26/90

- Rachel talked about anger, violence, and cursing. Two years ago she had a fight and cut a girl named Marie with a knife. Rachel said she preferred black men to whites. She started dating black men when she was sixteen. Mike, a white boy, had broken her heart. She really loved him. It took years to get over him. She said she'd never have a man again. She started dating Tyrone after this, and Mike's family was angry at her for dating a black man. Rachel had loved Mike and had given him her heart. After this, she closed her heart.

When Rachel arrived on the steps of Mercy Ministries, a war was raging inside her. She needed help in every area of her life, from her doubts, fears, and nightmares to her poor eating habits. Mostly she needed deliverance from her bitterness against those who had abused and violated her.

Despite her horrendous past, Rachel's life began to take a miraculous turn at Mercy Ministries. Through prayer and the teaching of the Word, she was able to forgive the people of her past. The Bible came alive to her.

Rachel's progress was steady. She had finally come into a life of joy in the freedom Jesus Christ had given. But once Rachel was on the road to real restoration, the ultimate fight for her soul began.

Rachel decided she was ready to leave the home. Her counselors agreed that she had improved but not to the point of maturity needed to live outside the home. We pleaded with her to stay. But she made her decision, and against the advice of the Mercy Ministries staff, Rachel left. We knew she wasn't ready.

Once it became clear that her heart was set on leaving, we tried to make the best of a bad situation. We advised her to enter a halfway house to make her society reentry process smoother. She agreed but only stayed a few weeks. In an attempt to keep her from drifting further away, we encouraged her to move in with a Christian family that not only graciously provided her a place to stay, but gave her a job in the family business. We hoped for the best but were still concerned.

Despite our efforts to help and the influence of the family she stayed with, Rachel was descending toward destruction. Although she had tasted the good life, she longed for the old. She disregarded the guidelines set by her new family and stayed out till all hours of the night with non-Christian friends. Finally, the couple explained to Rachel that despite their love and their desire to see her prosper spiritually, they had a responsibility to their own children and if she could not abide by the rules laid out for her, she could no longer stay.

Instead of repenting, Rachel left. She knew she was returning to what she had been freed from, but she claimed she could wait until later to get her life straightened out. "I'm just not ready yet," she said.

A few months later I received a call from my sister. "Nancy," she said, "I've just heard some terrible news. Rachel has been murdered. They found her body. It's awful what was done to her."

My knees nearly collapsed under my body as my mind caught up with my heart.

As we later found out, Rachel had returned to her mother's home. She had always had an underlying need for her mother's acceptance. At the urging of her mother, Rachel married someone she had just met. Four months later, on a Wednesday, her new husband reported her missing. That Friday she was found tied up in a field. She had multiple stab wounds and head injuries. It looked as if a hollow steel pipe had been pounded into her head, face, and chest. The man she married was later arrested and charged with Rachel's murder. He is rumored to be a Satanist.

The agonizing reality that Rachel had had the opportunity set before her to have abundant life haunts me often. Every day I encounter girls who live nightmares like this, and I have no guarantee they will come out serving God. What I do have is a calling to serve God and to do His work no matter what the cost, no matter what the loss.

Amazingly, the vast majority of the young women who come to Mercy Ministries do find restoration. They make the choice to live God's way, and their lives are totally transformed by the power of the Gospel. After they leave the homes, they go on to lead stable and mature Christian lives. Despite their struggles with pain, doubts, and temptation, they persevere in this thing called abundant life.

These girls are my heroes.

6

My Heroes

Lives That Have Been Restored

For I was hungry and you gave Me food; I was thirsty and you gave Me drink; I was a stranger and you took Me in; I was naked and you clothed Me; I was sick and you visited Me; I was in prison and you came to Me. Assuredly, I say to you, inasmuch as you did it to one of the least of these My brethren, you did it to Me. (Matthew 25:35-36, 40)

"Hello and welcome to 'Heart to Heart.'"

Sheila Walsh sat across from me, looking into the camera as she opened her daily television show. "We hear about troubled kids and runaways and unwanted pregnancies all the time. But perhaps many of us shake our heads and hope that somebody else will take care of it. Well, my guest today is involved as part of the solution. Let's take a look at what she does."

After a film clip of a service where I spoke to raise funds for a home in Nashville, Sheila continued her introduction: "And since opening facilities for females with various needs, Mercy Ministries has cared for almost a thousand girls. In the past five years, its home for unwed mothers has placed at least sixty babies for adoption. Please welcome from Nashville, Tennessee, the founder of Mercy Ministries, Nancy Alcorn."

As the camera caught us both in its frame, I felt like a vessel, ready and willing to be used. I was not there for people to see Nancy Alcorn. Instead, it was a golden opportunity for people to see what Mercy Ministries is really about—the young women who live there.

As Sheila questioned me about Mercy Ministries, the anxieties left and God's peace flooded my heart. As we talked about the girls whose lives had been touched and changed through Mercy Ministries, I wanted to use this opportunity to encourage the faith of these young women.

"I know they're listening to me today," I told Sheila. "I'm proud of them. My heroes are not the great tennis players and the basketball stars even though I'm a sports nut. My heroes are those girls. They come and go through the program, and many times go through the shame of carrying a child when it would be so easy just to sweep it under the rug and not tell anyone. But they're willing to leave their pride and selfishness behind and choose life. Those girls are my heroes, and I love them."

My feelings have not changed. They are still my heroes. Their lives have been touched by trials and battles I cannot imagine enduring. And not only have they lived these nightmares, but they have become conquerors of their fears through the gentle comfort of the Holy Spirit. Some of the girls have dared to have babies out of wedlock in this point-the-finger society. Others have renounced their past, placing their trust in the God of their future. Still others have done the seemingly unimaginable—they have forgiven the people who have caused their pain. Rather than hating them, they now pray for them.

To see their struggles and have the honor of being a part of their victories makes me stand in awe of their courage and of the incredible restoring power of God. Because of this, they are my heroes, and these are their stories.

Rhonda

From as far back as she could remember, Rhonda endured both physical and sexual abuse. By the time she was four years old, she was taken from her home because of the abuse she had suffered. Though removed from the situation, the experience remained. Her early suicide attempts seemed inevitable.

Growing up, she was tossed from one state psychiatric program to another and was shuffled in and out of foster homes and correctional institutions. No treatment program could heal the wounds. No foster program could offer the much needed stability. No correctional institution could offer her true freedom. Her situation became worse as she grew older. The pain she had been through as a child was manifested in bitterness and rebellion. A life of lesbianism offered protection from the abuse embedded in her mind.

Rhonda grew to be six feet, two inches tall. To escape the painful reality of her past she began hiding her insecurities behind drugs, alcohol, and eventually, food. Rhonda grew to weigh over three hundred pounds, causing her to dress only in men's clothes. Her poor self-image led her deeper into a lesbian lifestyle—ultimately reinforcing her sense of hopelessness.

Rhonda eventually realized she needed help from an outside source and sought guidance from a local pastor. He could see by the look in her eyes that she needed a refuge—not only from her past but from the war in her mind.

But where could Rhonda go to find true freedom when she was so controlled by her addictions? Where could she go to find peace when all she had known was turmoil? Where could she go to find security when all she had known was insecurity? Through the wisdom of the Holy Spirit, the pastor knew where to send her. Rhonda came to Mercy Ministries. She came to Jesus.

Although she desperately needed to escape from her seemingly hopeless situation, Rhonda did not immediately agree to come to Mercy Ministries. Our rules forbid her from smoking and drinking, both of which she was in bondage to. But she ultimately feared failure. Perhaps you have felt this way at some point in your life. The feeling of trying yet again to make something positive happen only to see the winds of defeat claim your dream and your faith. In the past, so many places that were supposed to have helped Rhonda left her feeling helpless. Why should Mercy Ministries be different from all the other places with good intentions and fruitless efforts?

Despite her doubts, Rhonda realized that her life would not change by itself. By the time she left our care, the only way I can describe her is to say that she was one of the most gorgeous young women I have ever seen! She lost over a hundred and twenty-five pounds, changed her glasses to contacts, and replaced the men's clothes that had once offered security with clothes fitting of the woman she had become. But beyond these remarkable changes was the amazing difference we saw in her face. A face shows a glimpse of the heart, and Rhonda's face was hardened with bitterness and despair when she arrived at Mercy Ministries. When she left, however, her countenance reflected the joy and peace only found in a relationship with Jesus Christ.

We had been allowed to witness her transformation from being an overweight, bitter, frightened child into a beautiful, forgiven woman of God. Lesbianism was part of her past and had been replaced with a pure life-style and Godly male friends. Most incredibly, although the physical change was so overwhelming, the change in her heart could bring a person to their knees. This was a heart that had been hurt at the hands of man and then healed by the hands of God.

After witnessing many such transformations by the grace and mercy of God, I, too, am often brought to my knees as I try to understand fully the awesome love of our holy and righteous Lord.

Rhonda now lives in Monroe, offering to others the selfless love offered to her. She takes meals to the elderly and works with a prison ministry. She still visits Mercy Ministries from time to time to volunteer her time to the place that changed her life forever.

Rhonda is one of my heroes.

Chris

A Christian heritage does not guarantee that a person will turn from a life of sin. Chris is a classic example of this sad reality. She was raised in a Spirit-filled home where Christ was worshiped as Lord and Savior. When I met Chris there was nothing about her that suggested she had ever heard of Jesus Christ or His love.

Chris is a beautiful woman. The hardness of her face, however, vividly revealed the life she had lived. By age thirty, she was pregnant for the fifth time, had already had two abortions and two miscarriages, and had been married three times. She seemed destined to spend her life on the road to destruction and ruin.

Chris had once owned a beauty salon, but she lost it due to her irresponsibility. She was too caught up in her life-style of heavy cocaine use and illicit sex to worry about anything other than her own wants and desires. After losing the shop, Chris managed to pay her bills by working at other salons. Yet, her drug use and violent temper robbed her of the opportunity to hold a steady job. Once she even beat up another employee.

Her fifth pregnancy led an unsuspecting Chris into the arms of a waiting Savior and to Mercy Ministries. She had scheduled a visit to Planned Parenthood for her third abortion. "Why not?" she thought to herself. "I've been doing so much cocaine, the baby will probably be deformed anyway."

Chris did not need Planned Parenthood. But where could she go to have a face-to-face encounter with God and a realization of her sin? Where could she go to find an alternative to abortion? Where could she go to find people who would pray with her and give her spiritual guidance despite her strong will? Chris came to Mercy Ministries. She came to Jesus.

One day, while struggling with the consequences of her sins, she picked up the phone. "Dad, it's me." As she told her father of her intentions, tears flowed on both ends of the phone. He pleaded with her not to go through with the abortion. "Chris, your mother and I are praying for you. God will bless you if you do what is right. Please don't do it this time!"

Chris sobbed as he told her about a place that offered the help she so desperately needed. "I know of a woman who has a place called Mercy Ministries. They help girls like you. She came to our church one Sunday and told all about it, and I *know* she can help you. Can I send her to talk to you?"

Chris agreed to the meeting but refused to cancel her appointment with Planned Parenthood.

I'll never forget that morning. It was early, and I was on my way out the door when the phone rang. Chris's dad related her story to me. I sensed the urgency and knew that this was a meeting only God could have arranged.

I knew I would encounter resistance from Chris, but I also knew the power of God could change her heart. I called our staff together to pray. I felt the Lord urging me to bring one of the girls who had been through the home for unwed mothers and now worked for Mercy Ministries. I believed Chris might see herself in the life of this girl.

When we arrived at Chris's apartment, the tears had ceased, and the wall she had built around herself dared us to enter. Though she was cordial, she obviously had no desire to hear our message. After talking with her a while, we knew we were not going to get through to her at this time. As we left, we silently prayed that something we had said would eventually seep through the cracks and invade the pain of her past. She thanked us for coming but said she was still planning to have an abortion.

As if the Holy Spirit grabbed my tongue, the Scripture of

Matthew 10:19— "Take no thought what ye shall speak: for it shall be given you in the same hour what ye shall speak" (KJV) was placed into action. "Chris," I said, reaching into my purse, "maybe we're not going to be able to help you, but we just got this video back. We're really trying to come up with some effective ways to reach people with situations just like yours. Would you mind taking a look at it and telling us if you think it would be an effective tool?" The videotape was from a Mercy Ministries "Celebration of Life" rally and included testimonies of people whose lives had been changed through their relationship with Mercy Ministries.

"I guess so," said Chris, "You came here to talk to me. The least I can do is watch your video."

I popped the videotape into her VCR, raised a "thank-you" to heaven, and continued to trust that God was somehow working in this situation. Music from a popular contemporary Christian group played, then testimonies were given by girls and families who had believed there was no hope for their circumstances until God showed them that He is the author of hope. Then, as pictures of babies who had been born and adopted through our ministry flashed on the screen along with a brief glimpse of an aborted fetus, Chris's hardened heart broke under the tender touch of the Holy Spirit. She watched until the tape ended. Finally, almost in a whisper, she asked the questions that haunt so many who fall by the wayside in our fallen world: "Do you really think there is hope for me? Do you really think I can change? Do you really think God still loves me?"

Chris didn't go to Planned Parenthood that day. Five days later she arrived at our home in Louisiana.

Yet, even though she had agreed to go to Mercy Ministries, she was still strong-willed. When she arrived, the first thing she told our staff was, "I didn't come here for you to try to save my soul. I came here for you to save my baby." She had resolved not to be changed during her stay at Mercy Ministries. Often though, our plans and God's plans are very different.

Instead of arguing with Chris, we offered love and understanding and left everything else to the divine intervention of the Lord. We felt it was a major victory that she had decided not to abort her child. We thought that, perhaps, as she grew more comfortable with her surroundings and gained a greater knowledge of the Gospel, her attitude would soften. "In her mind, she's come here for only one reason," we prayed, "but, Lord, we trust that You have brought her here for another reason as well."

Although we knew the Holy Spirit was working, we saw no evidence of a change in Chris. In fact, her attitude grew worse each day. As she participated in the Bible classes and attended prayer sessions, Chris became increasingly hostile and cynical. She lost her temper more than once, leaving few words unspoken as she released her colorful vocabulary on our staff members. Something had to happen.

Finally, we felt we had to confront Chris about her actions.

"Chris, the reason you are so miserable is because the Holy Spirit has you under conviction," we told her. "The reason you are under conviction is because an unholy heart cannot come into the presence of a holy God without coming head-to-head with the reality of its sin. We've all sinned, Chris. Not one of us here is exempt—we simply quit fighting His love and accepted it as something that is freely given. He doesn't care how many abortions you've had, or how many men you've slept with, or how many needles have penetrated the veins in your arms. He cares about you, about your hurts and your pain, and about your dreams and your future. He wants to forgive you. Not because you deserve it, Chris, but because He loves you."

Miraculously, the walls fell, and for the first time our words fell on listening ears.

"You're going through what King David talked about." We often tell the girls about David's escapade with Bathsheba— how he saw something he liked that belonged to someone else. He took it and used it for his pleasure, then tried to destroy anything that stood in the way of his own pleasure.

Listen to how David prayed to God:

> There was a time when I wouldn't admit what a sinner
> I was. But my dishonesty made me miserable and filled
> my days with frustration. All day and all night your
> hand was heavy on me. My strength evaporated like
> water on a sunny day until I finally admitted all my sins
> to you and stopped trying to hide them. I said to myself,
> "I will confess them to the Lord." And you forgave me!
> All my guilt is gone. (Psalm 32:3-5 TLB)

We read to her what David said: "What happiness for those
whose guilt has been forgiven! What joys when sins are covered over! What relief for those who have confessed their sins
and God has cleared their record" (Ps. 32:1-2 TLB).

The Holy Spirit finally broke through. Chris realized
Jesus' promise that "if we confess our sins, He is faithful and
just to forgive us our sins and to cleanse us from all unrighteousness" (1 John 1:9). Gradually we began to see small
changes occur. Every day was a new victory in Chris's walk
with Christ. The past that she could not forget was now forgiven. The temper that had lost her jobs was now controlled
and under submission. The staff that she once so rudely
addressed had now become her friends, her prayer partners,
her mentors. The other girls, who called her "Miss Know-It-
All," now saw a changed heart that was eager to learn. She
developed a hunger for the Word and invited every opportunity to learn more about the Lord. She consumed herself with
Bible classes, the Word, and teaching tapes.

God continued to prove Himself to Chris. One incident
involved direct intervention. On our first visit to Chris's apartment she had allowed us to pray for the health of her unborn
baby. With her constant drug use, deformity of the fetus was a
very real possibility. However, as Chris grew in her new life, her
child also grew. In answer to our prayers, an ultrasound showed
that the baby was completely healthy. Chris decided to leave our

home to live with her parents two months before the baby was due. She felt God clearly guiding her to keep her baby.

One month prior to her due date, Chris's water broke. Chris's first reaction was fear that it was too early. We learned, however, that if the baby had not been born at that time, it would have been born dead. The umbilical cord had wrapped itself around the baby's neck, and there was no room for additional growth in the womb. The baby would have eventually suffocated. The doctor could not explain why her water had broken early, but Chris knew God was answering a prayer prayed from an earnest heart.

After the birth of her son, Chris knew it was time to find a job. She decided to go back to the beauty salon from which she had been fired. When she arrived, she told her former boss, "I know I look like Chris, but I'm not the same person who used to work here. I'm changed." By the time she finished sharing her testimony, the woman was in tears. The same lady who had fired her rehired her, and Chris was shown another demonstration of God's restoration.

Since then, Chris has led several Bible studies with her fellow workers. I have been privileged to attend a couple of these meetings and have left each one deeply moved by Chris's simple yet elegant presentation of the Gospel message. As a result of Chris's boldness for Christ and her willingness to put her life with all its mistakes in other people's view, many people have realized God can change them too and have become Christians.

Chris became the top hairdresser in her salon and was able to give a portion of what she made each month to Mercy Ministries so other young women can receive the same help she was given. Chris occasionally accompanies me to churches to share the dynamic story of God's grace in her life and her incredible transformation. She now has a beautiful relationship with her family—God has truly restored Chris.

Chris is one of my heroes.

Jody

Tired of the abuse she endured at the hands of her family, Jody left home at age thirteen. By the time she was fourteen, she was a ward of the state. Much of her life was spent in and out of foster homes, orphanages, and correctional facilities, none of which offered the stability or positive values she needed.

Despite her chaotic upbringing, Jody managed to complete high school with grades high enough to be admitted to college. At the university, she met a man who promised her the world: the Casanova of her dreams. But he took her away from her problems only to add new ones. They moved in together, and she soon discovered his real job—drug dealer and pimp. For the next two years, Jody was caught in the entanglement of prostitution.

In the midst of this hellish life, Jody discovered she was pregnant. She went to a local crisis pregnancy center for confirmation and to explore her options. The center was a pro-life ministry, and they explained to her why it was wrong to abort her unborn child. Thank God for people who not only talk about saving lives but offer alternatives. God worked in Jody's heart to make her receptive to what she was hearing.

But where do you go when you are living in the midst of drug dealers and mafia kingpins? Where do you go when your life revolves around satisfying the sexual desires of others at the expense of your own life? Where do you go when the only truth you know is a lie? Jody came to Mercy Ministries. She came to Jesus.

I often wonder how God breaks through the deceptive schemes of the devil. Then I remember that He is God, and He can do whatever He wants according to His perfect will. In this case God wanted Jody to be free.

The crisis pregnancy center that persuaded Jody not to have an abortion also told her about Mercy Ministries. Jody finally learned what a real home was. For the first time in her life, she experienced pure love. She experienced love in the way it was meant to be. She experienced salvation. Her love for the Lord brought her into a deep relationship with Him. She turned her back on her old life of immorality and turned her face to reality. After much prayer, she decided that it would be best to give up her baby for adoption to a lovely couple who were earnestly praying for a child.

As the time grew closer for her to leave, Jody was unsure of her next step. She thought of returning to college but was hesitant because of the temptations of her old life. We encouraged her to pray and seek the Lord's will. At the same time, I was praying for God to bring someone to Mercy Ministries to be a part-time computer operator. As I prayed about a computer operator, my mind kept resting on Jody. I had no idea why she stayed at the front of my mind. So finally I asked her, "Jody, do you know anything about computers?"

"Of course," she replied. "I was majoring in computer science before I left college."

Jody turned out to be so good with our computer system that we eventually hired her to work full-time as our computer operator and receptionist. She was an invaluable asset to the staff and her love for Christ is challenging.

Jody is one of my heroes.

Connie

With no idea of the turmoil that lay ahead of her, Connie walked out her parents' front door with a few essentials at the tender age of twelve. She had no intention of returning. She wasn't too concerned about her age—most people thought she looked older than she was, so she felt she could make it on her own. She soon discovered that how old you look and how old you are are very different. But Connie wanted to rid herself of her parents and live her own life. Her boyfriend had promised her the world. He was considerably older and took advantage of her naiveté.

Connie soon discovered that many people make promises they never intend to keep. Within a few short weeks, Connie was entangled in a web of drug dealing and prostitution. Her "boyfriend" turned out to be a drug dealer with connections in organized crime. He also made money by pimping Connie and several other girls he had promised to "take care of."

After months of living like a slave, Connie managed to sneak out from where she and her "boyfriend" were living. Unfortunately, her brief escape cost her a very high price. He sent word that if Connie did not return they—the mafia—would kill her best friend. Connie did not take them seriously. Shortly after the warning, Connie's friend was murdered. It was then that Connie knew she had to find help.

She found a local Christian ministry called Safehouse. Safehouse is an outreach for runaways and prostitutes who need protection until they can be sent out of the state to get help.

But where could Connie go to escape the serious threats on her life? Where could she go to find out what real life was? Where could she go to find the Giver of Life? Connie came to Mercy Ministries. She came to Jesus.

We accepted Connie for two reasons. First, to protect her physically and second, to protect her spiritually. She stayed with us for over five months. During this time she became a new creation in Christ. Still, the hard part remained: she needed to forgive those who had hurt her and realize that she was not to blame for the death of her friend. While at Mercy Ministries Connie resolved both conflicts. And while she was at the home, her parents also committed their lives to Christ. The Holy Spirit manifested the power of reconciliation to her entire family.

In an effort to leave Connie's past where it belonged, her parents moved to another state. As a result, when she left Mercy Ministries, she was able to go back to a new home with a new family and new heart. Now she is living like a normal teenager. Instead of being twelve going on thirty, she is fifteen going on sixteen. She is finally enjoying life as it is meant to be enjoyed by a fifteen-year-old. She plays school sports, is involved with her church youth group, and can taste the true pleasures of being a teenager.

Connie is one of my heroes.

Debbie

Debbie's story is a little different. She was raised in a Christian home and was a committed believer in Jesus Christ. She had always sought His perfect will for her life. As a young woman, she met and fell in love with the man of her dreams, who also was a Christian. They dated for four years, planning to get married when they were old enough. Debbie firmly adhered to God's standards of sexual purity and was saving herself for her husband.

Then she was raped.

Debbie had decided to spend the summer working at a Christian camp. One night as her friends were watching television, she went upstairs to bed. As she lay in her room, she heard someone enter. She assumed it was one of her roommates and did not bother to question the entrance. A man came over to her bed, jumped on top of her, covered her mouth with his hand, and violently raped her. The wounds Debbie suffered that night went far beyond anything physical, and the horror of the ordeal lingered.

Shortly after the rape, Debbie learned she was pregnant. She had always believed abortion was wrong, that no matter how a child is conceived, it is still a life and to abort it would be murder. Yet her mind raged against the injustice of this event—this man had *raped* her. Furthermore, he had taken her virginity, which she could never replace and could never offer to her husband. The battle continued to torment her. The knowledge of the heart can often be overruled by the battle in the mind. She had to find a place to receive Christian guidance. She needed peace and emotional healing from the wounds that were so deeply scarring her discernment.

Where could this young girl go who had been so unmercifully violated? Where could this girl who had saved herself for one man—a man who now rejected her—go after this unspeakable act? Where could this girl go who was questioning the very foundation of her faith and the Creator she had so passionately served? Debbie came to Mercy Ministries. She came to Jesus.

When she arrived at the home, we knew there was one thing Debbie needed and that was love. So we took her in our arms and loved her unconditionally. We also let her know that rape was not a sign that God was punishing her or that He cared any less about her. Instead, it was a sign that the enemy was out to steal, kill, and destroy, and if she would let him he would destroy her.

She did not intend to let the devil destroy her. She focused instead on finding the will of God for her unborn child. She wrestled for a while over whether to keep the baby or give it up for adoption. She finally decided it would be best to give it up for adoption. She wanted to meet the adoptive parents to be sure they would provide a loving home. Under the circumstances I agreed with her decision. As she placed the child that was a part of her in the arms of a family that had so longed for this day, the Lord gave her perfect peace. Tears were shed, of course, but she was watching a beautiful life that had been conceived in violence being brought into a realm of supernatural love. Although the baby was no longer in her arms, it was forever in her heart.

Debbie still struggled with one troubling issue, however. She could not understand why the man she had loved and wanted to spend the rest of her life with would leave her for circumstances she could not have controlled. I prayed for wisdom, knowing that in matters of the heart, we don't always see things clearly. I told Debbie that God had a man prepared for her who was even better than the one she had planned to marry. As ideal as she thought her old boyfriend had been for her, I told her the Lord had someone more perfect. I reminded her that God is faithful and does not want us to settle for second best in making the lifetime commitment of marriage. "Look at it this way," I said, "God wants you all to Himself right now, and the man He chooses to share you with will have to be one incredible individual."

Debbie left Mercy Ministries trusting God for her future, believing that it would be even better than before. True to His Word, God brought a young man into Debbie's life—a strongly committed Christian who did not reject her when she told him that she had been raped. They dated for approximately a year and were then married. Several of the staff attended the wedding to be part of Debbie's glorious joy. As a result of Debbie's resting in God's faithfulness, she now has a husband who will love her as Christ intended her to be loved and who will remain consistent even in the hard times.

Debbie is one of my heroes.

Sally

Though her features were beautiful, Sally looked so masculine that it was hard to tell she was a woman. She had lovely dark skin, big dark eyes with long eyelashes, and gorgeous dark hair. Nevertheless, she had managed to suppress her femininity to the point that her features went unnoticed. She didn't shave under her arms and had cropped her hair like a boy. She wore men's clothes and muscle shirts to proudly show off her bulk she had developed from weight-lifting. Every part of her was like a man, from her walk to the way she held her shoulders. She even shaved her face.

Sally was a lesbian, and the society she belonged to embraced her relationships. She was told that it was a perfectly valid alternative life-style, and she should feel no shame. She was consumed with the prevailing lie that says sexual orientation is something a person is born with. There's no point trying to correct your feelings, she was told, because there is absolutely nothing you can do to change your sexuality.

The message of the world, though acceptable to many, was not quite believable to Sally. Somehow in her heart she knew her sexual confusion was not perfectly natural. Although she had no knowledge of how to change, she desperately desired a new life.

But where does a woman go who has openly been with women and accepted other women with women? Where does a woman go to find help for her confusion: a heterosexual world that looks down on homosexuals or a homosexual community that sees heterosexuals as shallow and narrow-minded? Where does a woman go to escape from a reality that is not real? Sally came to Mercy Ministries. She came to Jesus.

Sally was referred to us by a street ministry she had contacted. The transfiguration of her life was not an easy process. On the verge of utter helplessness, she came to me asking, "Do you really think I can change?"

Sally was sincere, but her old habits continually held her back. She tended to put on masculine airs. Occasionally, I had to make her wear a dress to church instead of her usual jeans and T-shirt. The girls helped, offering to lend her their makeup and advice on how to fix her hair. Gradually, the Holy Spirit began His transforming work and she changed both inwardly and outwardly.

By the time she left the doors of our home in Monroe, she was a beautiful, feminine woman. She enrolled in Bible school and returned to her hometown after graduation. There she married a minister who is involved in the street ministry that had originally directed her to Mercy Ministries. Together, they have established a loving Christian home in which to raise their children.

Sally recently wrote me a letter in which she said, "Thank

you, Nancy, for telling me I wasn't born a lesbian, and thank you for making me wear dresses to church. Now I love to wear dresses, and I love it when my husband tells me I look beautiful in them. I love being a wife and mother."

What an awesome God we serve.

Sally is one of my heroes.

Cindy

One would never believe that Cindy, with her wealthy, upper-middle-class background, had suffered physical and sexual abuse as a child. She did what many consider doing when they deal with this kind of mental and physical torture: she tried to kill herself with a gun. Instead of shooting herself in the bedroom—she didn't want to mess up the carpet—she shot herself in the closet. She pulled the trigger. The bullet entered her head, where it remains today. One might think an incident like this would shake a family into realizing that they need help. But not Cindy's. Her father offered advice instead of comfort: "Shoot yourself in the mouth next time."

With nowhere else to turn, Cindy entered a spiral of destruction. Drugs became her god. She would do anything for a fix: offer her body, use dirty needles out of garbage cans, anything for a moment's escape from her agonizing reality. Her promiscuity intensified. Her sexual cravings led her to abort five babies.

Cindy was really searching for love. Finally, as if her luck was changing, she met the man she had so longed for. For the first time, she found someone who loved and cared for her, not for her body. They set a date to be married. The dream, however, came to an abrupt end when the two of them were in a motorcycle accident. Cindy survived, her fiancé did not. Cindy was devastated. The one love that seemed stable in her life had been taken from her, and she was alone again. She had literally hit the bottom rung on life's ladder.

Where could this upper-middle-class white girl go without

being judged? Where could someone who seemed to have everything but who really had nothing go? Where could this girl go who had to live a charade in order to hide the sins of the people who were supposed to love her? Cindy came to Mercy Ministries. She came to Jesus.

Referred to us by a city ministry, Cindy came to Monroe to try to put the pieces of her life back together. Within three weeks, after severe withdrawal from cocaine addiction, she was a conqueror. More important, she found forgiveness and restoration in Jesus Christ and was miraculously confirmed to be HIV negative.

Unless one knew her past, one would never know what a horrible life she has lived. One would never be able to see the scars from the sexual abuse she had endured and her past drug addiction. When people see Cindy now, all they see is Jesus.

What an amazing testimony of God's grace she is. To see her countenance is to see a woman transformed by an ever-amazing God.

Cindy is one of my heroes.

Sharon

Sharon wanted out. She knew her life of lesbianism and alcoholism were not how she was meant to live, but she was not having success on her own. She turned to a local Twelve-Step program for help. They could no more help her than she could help herself. They told her the program could help control her habit but that she would always be addicted. However, I am a firm believer that God can bring freedom from *any* addiction.

Sharon wanted total restoration but had no evidence that restoration was possible. She needed a place where faith could be birthed in the knowledge that Jesus Christ "forgives all my sins and heals all my diseases" (Ps. 103:3 NIV). She needed a place that boldly professes that there is a real and permanent deliverance from the demons that enslaved her.

But where could a woman go who didn't even know about

this Jesus? Where could she go to find someone who thought her lesbian life-style was not a matter of genetics? Where could a woman go who thought that if she slipped and took one drink, she was doomed because she would always be an alcoholic? Sharon came to Mercy Ministries. She came to Jesus.

God knew she needed Mercy Ministries. He placed a person in the Twelve-Step program where Sharon had tried to get help who led her to our Monroe home to begin restoring what Satan had tried to steal. There, Jesus Christ completely changed her life. Her confusion over her sexuality was replaced by a healthy and biblically—based sexuality, and she was set free from her bondage to alcohol.

Sharon's testimony and transformed life were a dynamic witness to her family. The Lord even gave her the privilege of being a tool of the Holy Spirit to lead her father, mother, and brother to a saving knowledge of Jesus Christ.

Upon completion of the Mercy Ministries program, Sharon was dealt more harsh blows. She lost her father to cancer and her brother to AIDS, but her faith remained unshaken. Instead of turning to the old means of comfort in the midst of her grief, she turned to the Comforter, the Holy Spirit. In the midst of her pain, she was blessed to see both their lives restored by Jesus Christ. She took comfort in the knowledge that though they were dead, they would live forever with their Savior.

Sharon later prepared for full-time ministry with Christ for the Nations in Dallas, Texas. Through their excellent program she learned about evangelism and street ministry. The Lord opened doors of ministry to her in New Orleans during Mardi Gras. She also visited one of the Mercy Ministries' homes, not as a former resident, but as an invited guest speaker, giving God all the glory for her deliverance.

Sharon is one of my heroes.

Carrie

Born and raised in a devout Christian home, Carrie was a model child. She had made a decision that Jesus was Lord of her life and that this life He had given her would be used for Him. Then she went to college. It was only one date. It was only one night. It was only one time. But it only takes once.

The scenario will probably sound familiar. He was a good looking and charming "big man on campus." She was a young, naive college freshman who wanted to be accepted. They went out one night. She knew he was a non-Christian, but it was only one date. That one-evening date kept them together until morning. She had had no intention of sleeping with him. She had had no intention of it turning out the way it did.

As she got back to her dorm room, she dropped to her knees in sobs of utter repentance and asked the Lord for forgiveness for her mistake, for her sin. She vowed to never see him again.

But it didn't stop there.

That one night of pleasure had cost Carrie a lifetime of change: she was pregnant. When she discovered the frightening truth, she knew abortion was out of the question, despite the reaction she would have to endure from her family and peers. Should she keep the baby or should she give it up for adoption? Should she drop out of school and try to find a job? She needed answers.

But where could she go to receive unbiased advice? Where could she go now that her plans and dreams had turned into an unresolved nightmare? Where could she go to restore her faith in the God of her salvation? Who would encourage her faith as she walked the road she had paved from one careless evening? Carrie came to Mercy Ministries. She came to Jesus.

At Mercy Ministries, Carrie was able to accept the fact that God had forgiven her that morning on her dormitory floor. She further resolved to live her life for Christ, made a personal commitment that sex is for marriage, and decided to date only Christian men who had the same commitment. But her strongest resolve came when she decided to place her baby in the home of a childless couple. This couple now has a beautiful baby girl, and Carrie has a beautiful testimony of God's redeeming love.

After leaving Mercy Ministries, Carrie returned to college, remaining firm to her commitment. After several months, she met a fine Christian man through a campus outreach ministry. After they had dated for six months, Carrie gave me a call.

"Nancy," she said, "I really believe that this guy is the one God wants for me, but I was wondering if I could bring him over and let you check him out and see what you think of him."

I laughed, "That would be great!" I told her, "Bring him over." The high honor and important responsibility of meeting and approving Carrie's boyfriend as a possible husband made me feel like a mother. I felt privileged that my approval mattered.

When they came over, I "checked him out" and found him to be a committed Christian and a wonderful young man. He knew about her past but saw her through the eyes of a forgiving Jesus. This is a true test of one's real love for another. We must all realize that if Jesus can forgive, who are we to cast stones? If a person can't forgive, he or she doesn't truly love as the Lord intends. I gladly gave this union my blessing.

Since then they have joined in marriage, and God has blessed them with two wonderful children. Carrie thought she was beyond restoration, but God did "exceedingly, abundantly above all" that she could ask or even think (Eph. 3:20 KJV). He gave her more than forgiveness. He gave her a loving husband. He gave her two beautiful children. He gave her a powerful testimony—a testimony of the mighty power of redemption that God so easily bestows on those who simply ask.

Carrie is one of my heroes.

Katie

Raised by Christian parents engaged in full-time ministry, Katie decided their faith was not for her. She wanted to try this thing called life on her own terms and with her own ideas. She became sexually involved with a man who promised the moon, but left her with a handful of dirt. Inevitably, she was soon pregnant and, also inevitably, was offered no support from Mr. Moon Promiser.

Brokenhearted and desperate, Katie wanted to get out of her situation. Abortion seemed her easiest alternative. She did not want this baby, and she was too young for the responsibility of caring for an infant. But, in her heart, she knew abortion was not the right way. If she was going to carry the child to term, she would need a place to stay and get the appropriate medical attention. Most of all, she needed to accept the unconditional love of Jesus Christ and His message of reconciliation and forgiveness.

But where could this girl from a conservative community go without being judged for making a mistake? Where could this girl whose parents were pillars in their church go without placing a stigma on their ministry? Where could this real girl with a real problem go to find a real solution? Katie came to Mercy Ministries. She came to Jesus.

Moments away from having an abortion, Katie changed her mind at the last minute and, through the prayers of her mother, chose to go to Mercy Ministries. There she received the constant love and Godly counsel she so desperately needed. After a lot of time and a lot of tears, she was eventually reconciled with the family and the faith she had despised. She also decided to keep her baby and trust God to provide the right husband and father.

Katie left Mercy Ministries and moved to another state to live with her sister. God opened a door for her to work in the office of a wonderful, Bible-believing church. Though her parents had at first been uncertain about her decision, their first glimpse of those little hands and feet made this grand-daughter the joy of their lives.

Through her work at the church, Katie met an upstanding man of God, the church's youth pastor. After several months of spending time together and praying for God's will in their lives, they were married. Their church and their families were thrilled. And so am I.

Katie is one of my heroes.

* * * * *

These are a few of the many heroes that have touched my life as they've passed through the doors of Mercy Ministries. Some come in with the weight of the world on their shoulders. Some come to conquer the world, or just to conquer us. Some come because they have to; some because they want to. But all come by the divine intervention of Almighty God. Not all leave in the condition we have prayed they would. Some never fully make a commitment to serve Jesus Christ with all their heart and soul and mind. But they all leave knowing that there is a God who loves them and died to save them.

Countless young women who spent time at Mercy Ministries are now happily married wives, joyful mothers, graduates of Bible colleges and missions schools, and servants in various ministries. I love them all and am so thankful that God allowed me the privilege of being a vessel in His hands to direct these girls to the saving knowledge of Jesus Christ.

Although God is the heart changer, He needs us to act as servants. Standing away from ministries of mercy because they seem to be fine the way they are can cause apathy in the church. Most people do not lack kindness or compassion for those who are hurting, but they leave it to others to do the hands-on ministry.

Many Christians are unaware of the tremendous need that exists among hurting girls and unwed mothers for tangible signs of God's mercy. Churches that admirably support missionaries to foreign countries are unaware of much of the dire need for help in their own communities, sometimes on their own streets. All the picketing and marches and sit-ins in the world make no difference to a young girl if there is no one to offer a positive alternative to her situation. She needs something that will meet her immediate need, not something that will affect a law ten years from now.

Scripture demonstrates special concern for women and children, who are particularly vulnerable to abuse. Women and children are more likely to become victims in a society that is immune to the ways of the Lord. God's way of safeguarding women and children is through the mature love and protection of Christians. The Bible repeatedly challenges the people of God to look after widows and orphans.

For all intents and purposes, many of the girls who come to Mercy Ministries are like widows and orphans. Many have been abused the most by those who were supposed to love them the most. Others have been deceived by the schemes of the enemy and exploited because of neglect by those who were meant to protect them. Some have rebelled against their families and left their protective surrounding, making themselves easy prey to the attacks of Satan. Some others have neither rebelled against their parents nor been abused or neglected by them, but have, nevertheless, been victimized by the enemy.

The ten women I have described are not the only ones who are hurting from the onslaught of the world, the flesh, and the devil. Space does not allow me to share the hundreds of cases I have encountered of rape, incest, child abuse, prostitution, drugs, violence, crime, occult involvement, lesbianism, and other tragedies. And there are countless more girls out there who desperately need the same restoration the young women I described have received. They are not all products of dysfunctional homes. These girls come from every sort of background.

The one thing these young women share is a need for the healing hand of Jesus to repair their broken lives. Some need love and mercy. Others need assurance that Jesus has truly forgiven them. Some need counsel to lead them in a stable and productive Christian walk. Many need to forgive the ones who caused their pain. Others require counseling on how to be a single mother. And some need to be bonded with loving Christian families that want to adopt a baby. But they all need the Lord's mercy in some tangible form.

They all need Jesus.

As I said, these women are not the only ones with broken lives. We cannot turn a glassy stare toward the detestable holocaust of abortion that has invaded this country, a country supposedly built on Christian ideals, principles, and faith.

I am confident that God is raising up people in the civil government to overturn the *Roe v. Wade* Supreme Court decision legalizing child killing in this nation. When that happens, we will face an even greater need to help unwed mothers. In the meantime, we can only save the lives of babies if we offer young women a positive alternative to aborting their children. Christians need to respond. We need to provide places where unwed mothers can go, free of charge, to have their babies and be allowed to choose between keeping their children and placing them in adoptive homes—homes where people are asking God to provide them with children. We need to give so unborn children can live.

We need to provide places where broken lives find restoration. Not just in Louisiana, but all over the country.

7

Bread from Heaven

Support of the Ministry

"Bring all the tithes into the storehouse, that there may be food in My house, and prove me now in this," says the LORD of hosts, "If I will not open for you the windows of heaven and pour out for you such blessing that there will not be room enough to receive it." (Malachi 3:10)

Mercy Ministries does not charge young women for staying in our homes, for the counseling they receive, or for the life-preparation training we offer. Part of the reason for this, of course, is that many of the girls who come to the homes do not have any financial means. What a tragedy it would be for a child to be killed because a young woman could afford an abortion but not a safe haven to have her baby.

Even more important to us, however, is our desire to represent the unconditional love of Jesus. There are quite a number of girls whose parents could pay to send them to Mercy Ministries. If we charged any of the girls, though, they would be tempted to think that we were trying to help them simply because we were getting paid for our services. We don't want to give the accuser any opportunity to cause the young women to doubt our intentions. Parents who are able to help us financially are welcome to make contributions, but we never require them to do so.

Life in the Kingdom

One of the principles we teach the young women is that of sowing and reaping. It is an important part of their development to understand that God has commanded us to give back to Him a portion of what we earn so that He may bless us for our obedience to willingly give to Him first. The girls have experienced firsthand His faithfulness to fulfill this promise.

Lisa learned from us that God wants her to give ten percent of her income back to Him. Her parents were sending her twenty-five dollars every two weeks and much of it was needed to cover basic necessities. She desperately needed new contact lenses but did not want to ask her family for the money. She knew it was even a struggle for them to send the twenty-five dollars. Lisa had been praying that the Lord would provide her with the contacts. Instead of hoarding her allowance, she faithfully gave back to God's work five of the twenty-five dollars each time she received it.

One Sunday after church, a member of the congregation made her way to me. She looked as though she had something important on her mind.

"Nancy," she said, "God has given me a burden to buy Lisa some glasses or contact lenses. Do you know which she would prefer?"

I smiled broadly. "That's wonderful!" I exclaimed. "Lisa has been praying for the Lord to provide her with a pair of contacts for a while now. She'll be so excited when you tell her He's put it in your heart to help her."

God used a sister in Christ to vividly prove to Lisa that He will indeed "open the windows of heaven" for those who "bring the tithes into the storehouse." She had been taught about sowing seed for her need, so she put into action what she had learned and God honored her faith.

Lisa is only one of many girls who have come to Mercy Ministries and have been dramatically changed by God in response to their obedience to the Christian principles of sowing and reaping.

Shannon began giving a portion of her meager spending money back to the Lord. Before she came to Mercy Ministries, she was heavily involved in the drug culture. In that violent situation, her teeth were knocked out by an abusive, drug-dealing boyfriend.

Shannon truly needed a new set of teeth to match the new life she had found in Christ. Instead of worrying or attempting to save every penny she could get her hands on, Shannon prayed and sacrificially gave from the little she had. Before long, the Holy Spirit moved on two congregations to pay for her new teeth and prompted a Monroe dentist to donate his labor.

Many people wonder how we are able to persuade the girls to tithe from their income and trust God for their needs. Probably one of the reasons is that we don't ask them to do anything we aren't doing ourselves. Mercy Ministries gives ten percent of all the money it receives to other ministries. While there are many times it seems we can't afford to tithe, God has convicted me we can't afford not to.

We take ten percent off the top before we even look at our bills. By personal example, we demonstrate to the girls that we really believe what Jesus taught: "Give, and it shall be given unto you: good measure, pressed down, shaken together, and running over, shall men give into your bosom. For with the same measure that ye mete withal it shall be measured to you again" (Luke 6:38 KJV).

Not only do we provide the girls with an example to follow, quite often the Lord enables us to demonstrate that He will indeed bless those who allow Him to rule their finances.

"I have a sin I need to confess," I stated at the beginning of a Bible class one day.

Silence filled the room as the girls turned toward me. They seemed both surprised and curious.

"The Holy Spirit has been convicting me," I continued, "about worrying. You see, my car looks like it is about to stop running, and I can't afford to keep fixing it. I've been reminding God that He needs to either get me a new one or supernaturally preserve this one. But despite all my praying, I've still given in to worry."

I looked around the room at all the girls. They were paying close attention to me.

"Worrying is a sin. We're not supposed to worry; we're supposed to trust God. I've confessed it to God and I wanted to confess it to you as well."

I had no idea at the time how much of an impact what I told the girls was going to have on their lives—as well as mine. At the time, I was just happy to have an opportunity to demonstrate that Christians are supposed to "confess their sins to one another" (Jas. 5:16 NIV), and that we are not supposed to worry but to "cast your burden on the LORD, and He shall sustain you" (Ps. 55:22). But God also wanted to demonstrate to the girls how He blesses faithfulness to Him.

About two weeks later I received a check for five thousand dollars written out to me personally from a couple in another state. A letter with the check explained that this was the first of several checks that were to be given to me personally and that I was to use the money to buy myself a new car. Not only that, but they recommended the type of car I should consider buying, and it was the same model I had been praying for! I was able to drive a brand-new car off the lot, totally paid for by this precious couple who had listened to and obeyed what they felt the Lord wanted them to do.

It was a joyful experience to be able to tell the girls how God had blessed me with this car. Such real-life examples of God's power in the lives of His people are immense faith builders for the girls who come to Mercy Ministries.

Proof of God's faithfulness is also evident in the lives of the many Christians who support us. Jim and Kathy

Edwards, who had been donating their direct mail services to us, are one example.

They sent contributions to us regularly and, while they were by no means the sole support of Mercy Ministries, they certainly made a substantial contribution to our growth.

For a time, we were going through extreme financial hardship. We had several thousand dollars worth of bills due, and it didn't look as though we were going to be able to pay them. I did the only thing I could do—continued to pray for provision and faithfully carry out the work of the ministry.

One night the phone rang. It was Jim Edwards.

After we exchanged greetings, he told me why he had called: "Nancy, you know how God's been blessing our company?"

"Yes," I replied.

"Everything had been running very consistently for several months now, and we've even made a little profit. Our clients have been very satisfied with our work, and we're still growing like crazy."

"Then, last month, things went kind of flat. We were expecting to sign a contract with a new client that would have been very profitable, and at the last minute, they put the project on hold. Then, on top of everything else, when I started reviewing our numbers, I realized we had lost a substantial amount of money. I called our CPA to come in and check over our books to find out what happened, and he couldn't give me a logical answer. It just didn't make any sense."

"Have you gotten everything straightened out?" I asked.

"Well, yes and no. That's why I'm calling you. As I dug deeper, the only difference I could see in what we've done lately is that we haven't sent the ministry any contributions in a couple of months. The Lord convicted me that we need to remain faithful to Him in the good times as well as the bad. I don't know what your circumstances are down there, but God has shown me that I'm to get a contribution to you immediately! We're over-nighting a check for twenty-five thousand dollars. I apologize for being remiss in our giving."

I shared with them the financial struggles we'd been experiencing and how timely their gift was. I also told them I knew God would bless their giving.

About two weeks later, Kathy called to tell me that a major client they'd been trying to get for months had chosen their agency over several other contenders. "Nancy, there is no way in the natural realm that we should have signed this client. We are a very small company compared with those they usually work with, and we had a lot of competition for their business. This contract is the biggest by far that we've ever landed, and it will literally change the destiny of our company! Jim and I know, beyond a shadow of a doubt, that we got this business as a direct result of our gift to Mercy Ministries a couple of weeks ago. God is so faithful to bless us above that which we can ask or even think!"

The Edwards' company expanded rapidly into a multi-million-dollar business, and about a year later the Lord opened a door for them to sell it to a large, publicly traded company in England. They gave a portion of their profit to Mercy Ministries.

The evidence of God's incredible faithfulness in fulfilling our financial concerns has made it much easier to teach the girls about God's faithfulness in other areas of life. Because the girls learn to follow the principles of the kingdom in finances, they also begin following the principles of the kingdom in friendships, career planning, and Christian leadership.

The principles of Christ's kingdom are the opposite of the way the world thinks: 'For My thoughts are not your thoughts, neither are your ways My ways,' saith the LORD. 'For as the heavens are higher than the earth, so are My ways higher than your ways, and My thoughts than your thoughts'" (Isaiah 55:8-9 KJV).

Financially, the world says that if you want more money you need to save all you can or make good investments. God says if you want more riches you need to give away what you have. That is why I began tithing the income of Mercy Ministries from the beginning. From the world's standpoint, this does not make sense, but from a kingdom standpoint, it is a sound investment.

Socially, the world says that if you want to have friends, you need to manipulate people to get what you want. God says if you want to have friends, you need to be compassionate and loving to others (see Prov. 18:24). This is a lesson many of the young women who come to Mercy Ministries desperately need to learn.

In career planning and Christian leadership, Mercy Ministries also sets an example of how God's principles work. When the girls express a desire to find their calling in life or to minister in some way, we explain to them how they are to go about attaining the position they desire. In the world, one attains a position by struggling for it and opposing anyone who stands in the way. In the kingdom, however, one attains position by taking part in humble service:

> Likewise you younger people, submit yourselves to your elders. Yes, all of you be submissive to one another, and be clothed in humility, for "God resists the proud, but gives grace to the humble." Therefore humble yourselves under the mighty hand of God, that He may exalt you in due time, casting all your care upon Him, for He cares for you. (1 Peter 5:5-7)

We explain to the girls that if they wish to be great in the kingdom, they must become servants of all. If they wish to be exalted, they must follow Christ's example and submit themselves to God and man in a spirit of humility.

We also teach the girls that it is the small responsibilities they already have that are extremely important for their future in the kingdom. If we are faithful in the very little, God will make us rulers over many things (see Matt. 25:14-30; Luke 19:11-27).

By setting an example of service to the girls, and not "being lords over those entrusted to you, but being examples to the flock" (1 Peter 5:3), we are able to show them that we take God's principles seriously. We are also able to point to how God has blessed Mercy Ministries and worked in the lives of the staff to prove that His kingdom principles work. Just as God first taught me how to work in other ministries before He gave me leadership over one, I tell the girls that God will promote them after they prove themselves faithful and able in positions of lesser responsibility.

Bearing One Another's Burdens

A question I am constantly asked is where Mercy Ministries gets its financial support. The majority of it comes from individuals, businesses, or churches that have seen the fruit of changed lives. The Lord also provides for Mercy Ministries through the girls we help. Although we don't charge them a penny for coming to the homes, they are used by God to raise support for our work while they are with us and after they leave to start their new lives.

Clair is one example of how God uses the young women to whom we minister to bring us support.

Clair was headed for disaster. Though she was a member of a Bible-believing church in a small town, Clair was drifting away from the Christian faith. She rebelled against her parents and began experimenting with alcohol and drugs. She drifted even farther away when she discovered that her father had been involved in an affair. To make the situation worse, at the age of fourteen she was raped.

Her pastor knew he couldn't stand by and watch her fall away—he had a responsibility to Clair and her family. At the same time, he knew he couldn't possibly give her the kind of intensive counseling she required to triumph over her trials. He felt an obligation to try to help her, but he couldn't do it alone.

Fortunately, he had heard of Mercy Ministries. After contacting us and persuading Clair that she needed to go to the home for troubled girls, he helped her fill out an application form. She came to our home hoping to get her life back together.

At Mercy Ministries, Clair had an incredible life-changing experience of the love and power of Jesus Christ. Her attitude and outlook on life were transformed by the Holy Spirit. The things of God were suddenly made central in her life. She became a new creature in Christ.

The pastor continued to work with her family, hoping to bring about reconciliation between them and their daughter. When he got word of the amazing changes that were taking place in Clair's life, he asked me to speak to his church about the vision of Mercy Ministries. I was happy to talk to his congregation but decided that my presentation would be more effective if I also showed them an example of the results of Mercy Ministries' work. Though Clair's stay at the home was not yet over, we gave her a week off to visit her home and share her testimony with her church.

That Sunday, after I spoke on the need for the church to help unwed mothers and troubled young women, Clair spoke of how God had changed her life and helped her family. Most of the people in the congregation had noticed Clair's absence but did not know where she'd gone. Many were not aware of the problems Clair and her family had been experiencing, and they were more than a little shocked by her testimony.

When she finished, the pastor received a special offering for Mercy Ministries. It was difficult for him to speak because he had been moved to tears by Clair's story. Despite being a very small congregation, I was overwhelmed by the size of the donations that we received that evening. In addition, the pastor announced that Mercy Ministries would become a monthly recipient of their outreach fund to missions.

Jody is another example of how God has brought support

to Mercy Ministries. When Jody discovered she was pregnant, she didn't know what to do. The staff of the local crisis pregnancy center told her about Mercy Ministries. She came to the home for unwed mothers and became a Christian.

After she had her baby, the crisis pregnancy center that had directed her to us asked her to speak at a fund-raising banquet. They were so moved by Jody's testimony and the transformation that had taken place in her life that they sent Mercy Ministries a gift. They were a small organization that relied completely on contributions for support, so we were amazed and blessed at the amount of their check.

Christians who have been touched in some way by Mercy Ministries are one of the many sources of our support. Through the young women we assist, the Holy Spirit has led us into contact with a growing network of churches, crisis pregnancy centers, ministries, and businesses that have been led by God to help advance the vision of bringing restoration to broken lives.

Katrina came to our home for unwed mothers and turned over her life completely to God. After much prayer and counseling, she released her child for adoption.

When she left our home, she was trusting Christ for her needs. God provided her with an excellent job as a flight attendant with a major airline. Katrina not only keeps in touch with us, she also sends contributions to Mercy Ministries to help further our work.

Katrina is one of many girls who have left the homes feeling a burden to help. These young women continue to send checks for the sake of girls who are in the same kinds of situations in which they were once trapped. Because we minister to the whole person, the girls who leave Mercy Ministries are usually self-disciplined and mature enough to hold down good jobs and make consistent contributions to our work. Their gifts are especially meaningful to us because they represent the fruit of transformed lives. When the girls leave

Mercy Ministries, they are grateful to us and we feel gratitude for them as well.

Often, God moves in unusual and unexpected ways to meet our needs.

One morning I spoke in a large church in Louisiana, and I took several girls with me to share their testimonies. It was a powerful service with a strong anointing of the Holy Spirit. The congregation was deeply moved. The altar filled with many who wanted to make a total commitment to God.

After the service, I was approached by an attractive young woman who asked if she could speak to me privately. We walked away from the others still standing around the sanctuary and she placed a beautiful diamond ring in my hand. It had been given to her by a man she had lived with before she became a Christian.

She was now married and had two children, but she had held on to the diamond. It had become a source of contention between her and her husband. She told me that while I was speaking God impressed on her that she was to give the diamond to me so more young women could be helped. It was appraised at around sixteen thousand dollars, and we were able to sell it and use the money just as she had requested.

Another time, in the early days of Mercy Ministries, I spoke at a Wednesday night service in a small church in Monroe. We had a large financial need at that time, but we sincerely believed that God would meet it.

The next day a man called and said he had been in the service the night before. He was from California and was just in town for a few days. He had decided to attend services at a local church chosen at random. When he heard me speak, he felt prompted to give us a contribution. Before he left Monroe, he brought us a check for sixty-five hundred dollars. Once again, God was faithful to meet our need by moving the heart of an out-of-town stranger.

The Test of Faith

Many times it seemed Mercy Ministries would never get off the ground. It did not seem possible that the funding would ever come in. It was during those times that I was tempted with opportunities to take financial assistance and compromise the principles God had laid on my heart: when I was offered funding in exchange for letting a couple adopt a baby, when support was extended to me on the condition that I only deal with one denomination, and when I was offered financial assistance from the state. If I had decided to accept these offers of financial help, Mercy Ministries really wouldn't have gotten off the ground.

The Bible clearly states that God's people must do God's work in God's way according to God's Word or they will not succeed regardless of how good their intentions are. Jesus understood how important it is to do things the way God wants them to be done. He came to save us by dying in agony on the cross. Satan offered Him the world instead and tempted Him to bypass the pain:

> "Again, the devil took Him up on an exceedingly high mountain, and showed Him all the kingdoms of the world and their glory. And he said to Him, 'All these things I will give You if You will fall down and worship me'" (Matt. 4:8-9).

Jesus refused to follow Satan's scheme, but instead remained faithful to His Father's will. As a result, "God has made this Jesus, whom you crucified, both Lord and Christ" (Acts 2:36), the "ruler over the kings of the earth" (Rev. 1:5).

It often seems that what God wants us to do is impossible. It is tempting to take roads that look like shortcuts and compromise biblical principles. As long as we remain in God's favor, nothing is impossible. If we lose God's blessing, however, everything is impossible—we will not accomplish anything we attempt, no matter what our motives. We must remain faithful to Him.

Although Mercy Ministries has never built up a savings account or had extra money, we have never had any bills go unpaid. Just as God miraculously provided for my needs when I first moved to Monroe, He has consistently supplied the needs of Mercy Ministries. Time and time again, He has proved Himself to be Jehovah Jireh—"The Lord who provides." Sometimes it has looked as though we were going to be late paying our bills, but that has never happened either. The owner of a local print shop that does most of our publishing work told us that, of all the churches and Christian organizations he does business with, we are one of the few that pays its bills on time.

While Mercy Ministries' primary goal is to help troubled girls and unwed mothers, as well as their babies and adoptive couples, we also desire to minister to the entire church. It is our vision that Mercy Ministries as a growing organization will be an example to all Christians of how God *can* and *will* do the seemingly impossible if we remain faithful to Him. Many times Christians are tempted to believe that simple trust in God is not enough to get us through the financial trials of our lives. But God is able to help us not only survive but achieve *success* in our endeavors if we serve Him without compromise.

That is the message and conviction of Mercy Ministries.

8

The Army of the Lord

How God Enlists Laborers

Just as there are many parts to our bodies, so it is with Christ's body. We are all parts of it, and it takes every one of us to make it complete, for we each have different work to do. So we belong to each other, and each needs all the others. God has given each of us the ability to do certain things well. (Romans 12:4-6 TLB)

"So what do you think?"

The gentleman to whom I had been showing the homes said he was impressed. He represented a sizeable denomination that I was hoping would share in the work by financially supporting Mercy Ministries.

"We would like to support you," he continued, "but there are a few things we need to work out."

"Like what?" I asked.

"Well, for starters, we'd want you to get staff members from our church." I listened in disbelief as he told me what I needed to stop teaching and what I had to start teaching in order to get his denomination's support.

Finally I told him, "I'm sorry, but Mercy Ministries is trying to bring denominations together. If we simply become the mouthpiece of your group, we will be excluding members of the body of Christ, and if we compromise what the Word says, God will not be pleased."

The Body of Christ

From the beginning I wanted Mercy Ministries to be a source for bringing Christians together. Jesus prayed that all Christians "may be one, as You, Father, are in Me, and I in You; that they also may be one in Us, that the world may believe that You sent Me" (John 17:21). Not only is Christian unity desirable, according to Jesus' prayer, it is necessary for the conversion of the world. We need to display our unity in Christ in order to lead people to Him.

The unity of believers is more than something Mercy Ministries promotes; it is something on which Mercy Ministries depends. Without strong support from all different areas of the body of Christ, we would not be able to minister effectively to the girls who come to the homes.

God has equipped His church to deal with the adversity the world can bring against it. He has given us all gifts with which we can overcome obstacles and bring restoration to broken lives. But God has not given all the spiritual gifts to any one denomination; He has given them to His church, which includes all believers, regardless of denominational labels. We need to support each other.

The homes are supported both in finances and volunteer labor from Christians across the country representing various denominations.

Gathering Together

Mercy Ministries has been helped in many different ways. Christians from all over Monroe volunteered to help renovate our first home. Doctors and dentists have given their time and expertise to provide medical care for the girls. People with various skills and knowledge have come to the homes to tutor the young women and help some of them prepare for the G.E.D. test. Other young women receive help in preparing for college or Bible school.

Pastor Sam and Becky Carr of Word of Life Center in Shreveport, Louisiana, are two of the many volunteers that have helped at the homes by serving as Bible teachers and in many other areas. I initially contacted them because I had been told they were unable to have children and thought they might be interested in adopting. Becky said they had just adopted their second child so they were not interested in getting another one right away, but she knew of a couple that did want to adopt. Becky assisted me in placing our first baby, and I called on her again and again because she was doing such a fine job. Becky eventually became our official Adoptions Coordinator for a time, and she placed babies in numerous homes across the country.

When Sam and Becky were ready to adopt their third child, it was extra special to me that God allowed Mercy Ministries to be the source to complete their family. I felt that God was giving back to them because they had given so much to help us.

Carol Bryant is another example among many of someone who has graciously volunteered both time and energy at Mercy Ministries. Not only has she conducted seminars with the girls on how to forgive and see themselves as God sees them, but she has given them tips on makeup and clothing, helping them learn to like themselves and their appearances. Carol has been a professional model since 1976 and has a wealth of information and expertise. Her experience as both a Bible teacher and a model enable her to be a powerful tool in the lives of the girls.

Avoiding the Poverty Mentality

God has dealt with me from the beginning days of Mercy Ministries about how He wants me to conduct myself in the business affairs of this ministry, and I have trained the staff to do likewise.

Too often, especially in ministries such as this where the bare necessities have to be provided for needy people, there is a tendency to expect individuals and businesses to provide professional services free of charge. God has cautioned me to avoid looking to anyone besides Him to meet our needs and not to approach business people with our hand out, but rather to approach them asking what their best price would be for provision of a particular service or purchase of a particular item.

It is not that we don't want anyone to give of their time or substance if they feel inclined to do so, but any gift that comes to us should originate in the heart of the person who is giving. People must decide themselves whether God is leading them to volunteer their services or give their products. If we employ manipulation tactics and put people on "guilt trips," we may get what we want, but it is not of God. People's hearts should be moved by the Holy Spirit to give—not by methods of entrapment.

In 2 Corinthians 9:7, Paul gives instruction concerning our giving: "So let each one give as he purposes in his heart, not grudgingly or of necessity; for God loves a cheerful giver." It is not of God for people to give "grudgingly" because they have been manipulated, or of "necessity" because a need has been presented and undue pressure is applied to force the giving. God's way is to let people give as they "purpose" in their own heart, according to what He is showing them to do.

Several years ago, when it became public knowledge that certain ministries were being questioned regarding their integrity and mishandling of funds, I decided to seek expertise to make sure we were in order and above reproach at Mercy Ministries. In so doing, I was told about an accounting firm in Shreveport that has much experience working with nonprofit organizations and ministries. I knew it would be costly to retain this particular firm, but I felt it necessary to have the best, so I contracted Steve Doss, who agreed to take us as a client.

Steve initially spent long hours setting things in order and advising us of needed changes. Then he began doing financial statements for us each month, and we began believing God for the extra money needed to pay him. Several months went by and we had not received a bill. I was concerned, so I asked my secretary to call Steve's office. He responded a few days later with a letter explaining that he appreciated the work we were accomplishing and that he wanted to contribute by providing his services each month free of charge. Over five years passed, and Steve continued to provide his services. We offered to pay him on numerous occasions, but he "purposed in his heart" to contribute to Mercy Ministries in this way. We are grateful for Steve, and God has blessed his business immensely.

We had a similar experience in seeking an attorney. We crossed the path of Joe Dixon, Jr., in Monroe. He is a highly respected community leader and family man, as well as an outstanding attorney. Joe, like Steve, "purposed in his heart" to provide legal services for Mercy Ministries, not because we asked, but because God moved on his heart.

These are wonderful examples of God's provision, but certainly God does not do things the same way all the time. God may want Mercy Ministries to hire a particular business because He wants to use us to meet their need. For example, we needed to have a big printing job done, and we wanted it done right. We approached a certain printing business that had a good reputation in our area, and we agreed on a fair price. They did the job and God supplied us with the money to pay them. We didn't know it until afterward, but these people were Christians who had been praying for a large job that week to meet financial obligations of their own. In this case, they provided us with a needed service, we provided them with payment God had supplied, and both our needs were met.

It is so important not to "put God in a box" but to be led by the Holy Spirit. He meets our needs, and we must operate according to kingdom principles so that a poverty mentality will not take over and choke the blessings of God.

Raising Laborers

God has worked in many other ways to bring the right people to the staff of Mercy Ministries.

As I began to realize that God had called me to expand the outreach of Mercy Ministries beyond Louisiana, I started praying for the Lord to send someone who could take my place at the Monroe homes and allow me to go elsewhere to raise up a new work. God answered my prayer in an amazing way.

Four years earlier, in 1984, I was introduced to Dr. Le Z. Walter. At the time, she had recently become a Christian. I first got to know her to see if she might be able to help Mercy Ministries in the area of administration, as she was highly trained and experienced in this area. In developing a relationship with her, God gave me the privilege of counseling her in her new Christian life.

Le appeared to have everything—material belongings, a doctorate, loving parents—yet there had been an emptiness, a longing that was not filled by any of her past achievements or possessions. Once she met Jesus, she had only one desire—to know everything she could about Him and His ways. Because her situation in Monroe included an abusive and non-Christian spouse, Le needed to relocate so she could better learn to know the Lord. While I was sorry she would not be able to aid Mercy Ministries with her administrative skills, I was happy that she was growing in Christ. I had no idea God would use her—and my ministry to her—in the future.

Le left for her home state and got a job with the Oklahoma State Regents for Higher Education, the coordinating body for all the public colleges and universities in the state. At the same time, Le became involved in a church that reached out to the surrounding community. The Lord prospered Le's work for the state, and by 1986 she was promoted to the position of Vice Chancellor for Student Affairs and was the first woman to hold a vice chancellor's position.

While she was living in Oklahoma, Le and I kept in touch.

Twice she came back to Louisiana and visited the Mercy Ministries' homes. To my surprise, she asked if there was any way she could come back and work for Mercy Ministries. I explained that I could only pay her a small fraction of the salary she was making with the State of Oklahoma, but Le was more interested in how she could best serve God than in how much money she could make. I tried to discourage Le, but she was convinced that God was speaking. I soon became convinced as well.

God caused everything to fall into place for Le to come to Mercy Ministries. In a depressed Oklahoma City real estate market, her house sold seven months after she moved, and it was rented all but three weeks from the time she moved to Monroe until it was sold. God also provided her with the new car she needed. Having professed to be an atheist in years past, Le was overwhelmed at God's goodness to her since becoming a Christian.

As Le learned how Mercy Ministries worked, her God-given skills in administration as well as her heartfelt love for the girls enabled her to run the homes with more and more efficiency. Having had an abortion numerous years before, and having also been delivered from severe alcoholism, Le had immense compassion for the girls. Le also had the ability to provide "tough love" when the situation demanded it. She knew it would bring good in the end.

After working side by side with Le for a year, I realized that the homes ran as smoothly when I was gone on a teaching seminar as when I was in Monroe. God's calling Le provided me the freedom I needed to devote myself to expanding Mercy Ministries to other parts of the country.

God has also sent us interns from various colleges and universities.

Jackie Dudek, for example, came to us as an intern from Pat Robertson's Regent University. After getting a bachelor's degree in sociology, she had served for four years as a probation officer with juvenile and adult offenders from Saratoga County Probation, New York State. In that position, Jackie told me, "In spite of the many caring professionals and countless programs, I saw the same people coming back through the system, falling into the same destructive patterns. As a Christian I knew that Jesus Christ was the only answer for these troubled lives, and a burden was placed on my heart to seek God's solutions."

This burden led Jackie to enroll as a master's student of counseling at Regent University "to pursue God's heart for the lost and suffering." During a ten-week counseling internship in 1988, we were blessed with Jackie's help. She was also blessed by the experience and told me she was "excited to see the power of God change lives and to see these once-broken young women in turn going on to help others come to know Jesus and experience His great love. The world's way offered no hope, but clearly God's ways have been proven as many young women are being helped and their lives are totally transformed by God's power and love."

We were so impressed with Jackie's abilities that we wanted her to return. I went to her graduation ceremony in Virginia Beach and offered her a position at Mercy Ministries. She immediately accepted my offer and was with us for some time. She still tells people that "the work of Mercy Ministries is the Father's heart."

Jackie is not the only student who has interned at Mercy Ministries, and hopefully, there will be more in the future.

Many times God raises up laborers from among those He originally sent to us for help. Once they become new creatures in Christ, the Lord equips them and prepares them to work in the office and help us minister to the other girls.

Kristy is one of those young women. She first visited her younger sister who previously came to us for help. At the time, she thought, "This is such a nice place for people who really need it," assuming that she could not possibly be one of those people. Kristy went on with her life. She was heavily involved in going out every night to clubs and drinking and dancing until she realized her life was going nowhere. Deep down she knew she was not living as she should.

Eventually, she came to the home for troubled girls and gave her life to Christ. God not only gave her a new heart, but He worked to restore her relationship with her family and also converted her father. Kristy's life changed dramatically.

As a result of the profound change in her life, Kristy had a deep desire to serve others. She began to help us around the office and did such a good job that we asked her to join the staff. At a later date, she was able to be our receptionist and computer operator at the homes in Louisiana. We sent her to take computer classes from the local university to further equip her in her position. Kristy was an asset to us in the office, and she shared her testimony with the other girls and before churches. She is one of the many young women who have come to Mercy Ministries in need of help and, after their lives have been transformed, end up helping us.

Ann came to us as an unwed mother with a sordid background of rape, suicide attempts, and drug and alcohol abuse. When she was presented with the Gospel, Ann went through a dramatic and immediate life change. She developed a strong commitment to Jesus Christ and had a desire to serve the needs of others; she wanted her life to count for something.

Even before she had her baby, Ann began giving us much-needed help around the office. She was an efficient and thorough worker who had a sincere desire to help. After releasing her baby for adoption, she continued to assist at Mercy Ministries and eventually became a part of the staff.

Ann did not remain at Mercy Ministries, however. She felt God's call to enter the foreign mission field. After much prayer, she joined Youth With A Mission and went to Brazil for training. Mercy Ministries helped her raise money for her support. She hopes to eventually do missions work outside the United States.

Not only is Ann one of the many girls who has kept Mercy Ministries going by helping in its day-to-day operations, she also shows how we are adding to the work of the whole church. Many of the young women who come to us leave to pursue a calling to full-time ministry or to work in foreign missions. Numerous girls have left Mercy Ministries and gone directly to Bible school. Young women like Ann prove that God responds to the investment of the church in bringing restoration to broken lives by blessing His people with an increase in fellow laborers.

The Christian Network

One of the ways Mercy Ministries helps the rest of the body of Christ is by linking up with Christians who try to help girls consider alternatives to abortion. Stacy came to a crisis pregnancy center with her life in a shambles. She responded to the divorce of her parents by rebelling and becoming sexually involved with a drug dealer. She was pregnant and desperately needed discipleship. The people who worked at the crisis pregnancy center knew about Mercy Ministries and were able to get her an application form.

Stacy is one of many young women who have been recommended to Mercy Ministries by a crisis pregnancy center. We regularly receive referrals from crisis pregnancy centers around the country that have convinced young women not to have abortions but need a place to send them during their pregnancies.

Jenny was brought up in a Christian family and was a member of a committed church. Despite her upbringing and the spiritual surroundings at her church, Jenny was enticed by the world. One night, after a high school football game, Jenny went out with a non-Christian. "What will it hurt," she thought to herself. "I'll only do it once. Nothing will happen."

She did not know how great the consequences could be from one night's sin. Jenny was pregnant.

Knowing that she had sinned. Jenny was beside herself with guilt. She confessed to her parents and to her pastor. Fortunately, her pastor had known about Mercy Ministries for quite some time and had sent money from the church as a part of its outreach budget. He knew Jenny needed to be intensively discipled and restored by people who could give her the time and care she needed.

When Jenny came to Mercy Ministries, she immediately repented and rededicated her life to Christ. She confessed her sin and made a commitment that sex is for marriage. After she had prayed about what she should do, Jenny released the baby to be adopted by a doctor and his wife who had not been able to have children of their own. She then returned to her family and her church to live a committed Christian life. Now she is finishing high school and plans to attend college. She is excited about knowing Christ and provides leadership for her church youth group.

Jenny's situation is not unique. Mercy Ministries has a similar relationship with many pastors around the country who refer young women to us.

Gaining an Advocate

One of the many ways God has helped us grow is by bringing me in contact with Christian leaders who are willing to give their time to help raise support through prayer, labor, and funds for Mercy Ministries. God had an interesting way of bringing me together with Cal Thomas.

Like most Christians, I had heard of Cal Thomas's radio commentaries and his syndicated newspaper column. When I heard he was speaking at a church in Nashville, I jumped at the opportunity to go. His presentation was enlightening and entertaining as well as confrontational and challenging. The following is an account of what happened during the question-and-answer period at the end of his message.

Someone from the audience went to one of the microphones. "Mr. Thomas, what do you think Christians can best do about abortion?"

Cal answered that Christians could fight abortion several ways, but he concluded his comments by highly recommending crisis pregnancy centers. "In fact," he continued, "I do fundraising events for them. I am speaking at benefits for crisis pregnancy centers all the time. I think that is absolutely the most important thing I could do with my time."

As he spoke, I felt my heart begin to pound.

"As a matter of fact," he went on, "it's my favorite thing to do. I love it. Any opportunity I have, I try to help pro-life causes."

As he continued to extol pro-life programs and tell how much he enjoyed working for them, I got out of my seat and walked to a microphone. I could hardly believe what I was about to do. What if he thought I was a nut? My heart was pounding, but I had felt that pounding before. I knew I was being prompted by someone bigger than me.

When he was ready for the next question from the audience, I said, "I really appreciate what you're doing to help crisis pregnancy centers. It is very important and very needed. But there is a step further we can take by providing a place for girls to go where they can not only have their babies, but become Christians as well. I've been involved in starting such homes in Louisiana and plan to establish more. I was wondering, if you enjoy doing fund-raising so much for pro-life causes, would you be willing to do a fund-raising event for us at a later time?"

Everyone in the audience laughed as I walked back to my seat. Cal just smiled and remarked, "Nothing like an aggressive Christian woman!" Everyone laughed harder at that. When the audience had settled down, he continued, "I would be happy to help."

At that point, the pastor—who is a strong supporter of Mercy Ministries—stood up and said, "Cal, I just want to say that we fully endorse Nancy and her ministry. This is something you can be proud to speak on behalf of."

That was my first face-to-face encounter with Cal Thomas, a man for whom I have great respect. We would eventually meet again.

* * * * *

These are only a few of the ways Mercy Ministries has been helped by Christians from different areas of the country and different backgrounds, traditions, and denominations. Perhaps another way God will bring more people to help in our labor is by moving them as they read this book.

Perhaps He is even speaking to you right now.

9

The Ripple Effect

Restoration of One
Brings Restoration to Others

Blessed be the God and Father of our Lord Jesus Christ,
the Father of mercies and God of all comfort, who comforts
us in all our tribulation, that we may be able to confort
those who are in any trouble, with the comfort with which
we ourselves are comforted by God. (2 Corinthians 1:3-4
NIV)

Twelve-year-old Lisa Will watched intently as I led the girls into church. It was 1982, and I was working for Teen Challenge as director of the troubled young women who were staying there. I didn't know Lisa except that she was the daughter of David Will, who sang with the Imperials, a well-known contemporary Christian music group. We attended the same church and had mutual friends, but I had never gotten to know David and his wife, or their daughters.

Lisa knew I worked with the girls at Teen Challenge and always watched me with them in church. "I wonder what those girls have done to end up there," she thought to herself. "I wonder if they're mean." She couldn't imagine what could possibly bring someone to the point of seeking out a home for troubled girls. Little did she know she would eventually be one of those seekers.

I left for Louisiana and lost touch with many of my friends

in Nashville. However, I stayed in contact with Sandy Sterban, a close friend of Lisa's mother, Jan. I never imagined how important that relationship would eventually be for Lisa and for the rest of her family.

Falling

When Lisa entered junior high school at age thirteen, she began to rebel against her Christian upbringing. She had seen hypocrisy in the church and used her disillusionment with Christians as an excuse to go her own way. It wasn't long before sneaking around behind her parents' backs became the norm. She began staying out until all hours of the night to attend wild parties and drink.

Her parents felt something was not right with their daughter, but the facade she wore had deceived even them. They prayed for her continually, trusting God to keep her from harm and restore her to Himself. Lisa knew they were praying for her. She was protected too many times for it to be coincidence. On more than one occasion when she was among friends who got in trouble with the police, she somehow managed to evade arrest. She was even involved in several automobile accidents with her friends and she came out barely scratched. Every time the devil sent danger her way, the Lord protected her.

Despite Lisa's desire to party, she loved her parents. She knew if they found out about the life she was living they would be devastated. For eight years she continued to live a double life, trying to find fulfillment through unfulfilling vices. One day, as she was in a bar with some friends, she met a man. Within three months of dating him, she discovered she was pregnant. She had to face a choice. If she stayed pregnant there was no way she could hide it from her parents.

Lisa decided to get an abortion—even though she knew it was wrong. She and the father tried to raise enough money for the procedure. Marriage was out of the question because she was not in love with him, nor he with her. At the abortion clinic, the doctor refused to perform the abortion because she was bleeding. The doctor said her body was trying to abort the baby—probably because of cigarette and alcohol abuse. A miscarriage seemed imminent.

She waited a few days, vainly hoping for a miscarriage. She decided to find someone who would perform the abortion despite her condition. She found a place in the phone book that gave free pregnancy tests. She went there only to discover that it was a pro-life crisis pregnancy center. As she sat through their video presentation, which left no doubt that abortion was murder, she knew her parents' prayers were following her once again—keeping her from aborting her child. As her girlfriend drove her away from the center, Lisa became so angry that she ripped all the pro-life literature she had been given into pieces and threw it out the window onto the highway.

Out of frustration, Lisa finally decided to tell her parents the truth. With her girlfriend present for moral support, she informed her mother and father that she was pregnant. David later said of that evening, "My heart sank as she told us the words every parent dreads to hear. We were not surprised. We had known for a long time in our spirits that something was wrong."

Nevertheless, David and Jan were extremely supportive and responded to her plight with love. Assuring her that they forgave her, they took her in their arms, and as the tears flowed, they prayed, "God, change our daughter."

They also told her they would stand behind any decision she made except deciding to have an abortion. "You're still our daughter and we still love you," said her parents. "If you want to keep the baby, we'll support you. If you want to give the baby up for adoption, we'll support you. But we won't support abortion."

Having chosen to carry the baby to term, however, neither Lisa nor her family knew how they should handle the situation.

The Way Home

While the Wills were wondering what course they should take, Jan called Sandy and asked her to pray for them that they could all get through this crisis. Sandy thought of Mercy Ministries.

"Do you remember Nancy Alcorn who used to go to our church and worked for Teen Challenge?" she asked.

"Yes. What about her?" asked Jan.

"Well, she's started a home for unwed mothers in Monroe, Louisiana, that takes in girls from all over the country free of charge."

"Really?" Jan sounded surprised.

"Not only that," said Sandy, "but they teach the girls from the Bible and disciple them to live for God."

After they contacted me, I sent Lisa an application to fill out. When she saw all the rules she was going to have to follow, she almost decided not to come. She had been living as she pleased for seven years. It was difficult for her to suddenly contemplate living in submission to authority. Nonetheless, she finally decided to come. I talked with her over the phone to be sure she understood everything. She told me she wanted to come to our home for unwed mothers because she knew she needed help.

Lisa's parents drove her to Monroe in May 1988. I'll never forget that day. David and Jan thanked me for taking her into the home. They were obviously upset. "We've known since Lisa was a baby that God had a call on her life," her father told me as his voice broke, "and we're believing that this is going to turn for good."

The Wills also told me that they had decided as a family not to hide Lisa's visit to the home. "I don't want to have to sneak around," said Lisa, "and pretend that I have gone off to see some relative for nine months." It was obvious that David and Jan wanted to be open about it as well. I was impressed with the way they were handling this crisis.

Their tears fell like rain as Lisa and her parents said good-bye to each other. As the Wills drove out the driveway to head back to Nashville, I vividly recall Lisa weeping as she looked out the window to watch them depart. It was heart wrenching to see how one decision could affect so many lives.

For the next couple of weeks, Lisa's life was difficult. She constantly talked about how much she missed her family, and then the tears would fall again. She didn't like being away from her parents' home. A couple of times she called her mom and dad, and they had to tell her Mercy Ministries was what she needed to make it through this time and not to give up. "You're where you need to be," they said.

Despite her parents' encouragement, it was obvious Lisa was miserable. None of us knew Lisa was still hoping she would have a miscarriage.

One day, in one of our classes, I was talking with the girls about how God could remove the chains that held them in bondage. The Holy Spirit impressed me to pray with those who sincerely longed to be free.

Four or five girls came to me, and Lisa was one of them. I prayed with her, asking God to enable her to completely yield herself and to give her perfect wisdom about His will for her unborn baby. As I prayed, Lisa broke. The Spirit of God spoke to my heart that Lisa was still secretly hoping that she would miscarry her child. Not wanting to embarrass her, I whispered in her ear that her desire to have a miscarriage was not pleasing to God. "If you'll just accept the situation as it is," I told her, "and ask for forgiveness for hoping the baby will die, then God can change your heart and give you perfect peace. He'll not only do something good for the baby, but He'll do something good for you as well." Convicted of her sinful attitude, Lisa cried even more heavily.

I whispered again in her ear, "God's not down on you. Just confess your sins and trust that He has forgiven them. I'd probably feel that way too if I were in your place." I prayed with her for forgiveness and the Holy Spirit comforted her.

From that time forward, Lisa's attitude was completely changed. Instead of being negative, she began to enjoy life in the home and became optimistic about her future. She loved the Bible classes as well as the teaching tapes and Christian books. She started putting the Godly counsel she was receiving into action.

When her dad would call Lisa from the road as he toured with the Imperials, he was struck by the significant change that had occurred in her attitude. It seemed as though she was constantly sharing new revelations from the Word. She would bubble over with enthusiasm saying, "Dad, Dad, you'll never guess what I learned today! You need to share it at your concerts."

Later, he called me and said, "I don't know what's happened to Lisa, but it is incredible! Whatever you all are doing with her, just keep on doing it."

"Well, God's the one doing it," I said. "You just keep praying."

At her next appointment with a Louisiana doctor, Lisa was told that she was doing much better and would probably be able to carry the baby to term. Instead of being disappointed with this news, she was happy.

As Lisa began praying that God would reveal to her His plan for her future, she started to practice singing. Lisa had always had a desire to become a singer but doubted the possibility of it ever amounting to anything. Little did she know how God would use that desire.

The Wills continued to refuse to hide what was happening in their family. They were open and honest about the fact that their daughter had gone to Mercy Ministries due to an unplanned pregnancy. Lisa wanted it that way—hoping people would learn from her mistakes. In fact, she asked her dad to share her story at his concerts to convict Christians in the audience who were living a double life. They all prayed that, by being transparent about what was going on in their home, other hurting Christian families would be encouraged, as the Bible tells us, to "confess your sins to each other and pray for each other so that you may be healed" (Jas. 5:16 NIV). David Will was able to minister to many hurting parents and children because of his daughter's willingness to share her message.

Sisters in Christ

Once Lisa was living for God, she began to feel a burden for Anjy, one of her younger sisters. During her morning prayer time she regularly asked the other girls and the staff to pray for her sister Anjy. While Lisa had been going her own way and living wildly, Anjy had also drifted from her Christian upbringing. Anjy became involved with a young man who was heavily involved in the occult. She began listening to his music and being influenced by him in other ways. Gradually her appearance and behavior changed. She wore only black clothing and used only black fingernail polish. To top it all off, she dyed her hair white.

The changes in Anjy involved more than just her appearance, however. Her usual facial expression became less pleasant and more sullen. She became afraid of sleeping by herself in the dark, and she would even see things move around in her room. Anjy became so scared that she would frequently come into Lisa's room and ask to sleep with her. If Lisa was out that night, she would sleep with her younger sister, Nicole. She could not bear to be by herself.

Lisa had not been happy with the boy her sister was dating. Nor had she liked the changes she saw in Anjy. Since Lisa was not living a life she could be proud of, however, she did not see how she could tell her sister to change her ways. But now that she had given her life to God, Lisa wanted to see her sister restored to the Lord. She felt somewhat responsible for the life her sister was living, realizing that she had set a poor example. Her personal choices had caused a ripple effect that had affected Anjy negatively. We all prayed with her, not knowing how we would be involved in the answer to Lisa's prayer.

A few months later, early in August, the Imperials had a concert at Six Flags over Texas. Realizing that Monroe, Louisiana, was only five hours from Dallas, Armond Morales—who is the leader of the Imperials—and his wife Bonnie asked us if we'd like to bring the girls to the park and the concert. If so, Bonnie would arrange for the tickets. We welcomed the opportunity, not only to give Lisa an opportunity to see her dad, but because we take the girls to Christian concerts and special events when we can.

Lisa and David were overjoyed to see one another after a long separation. Lisa ran to her father and threw her arms around him. It was incredible to see this father and daughter unified by their mutual commitment to Jesus Christ, especially after all they had been through.

The girls had a wonderful time, and I was grateful to the Imperials for providing us a chance to get away. Lisa's presence in the home had ministered to the other girls. While we were together, I got to know David and the rest of the Imperials better. I was planning to drive to Tennessee for the Labor Day weekend to visit my parents, so I talked with David about bringing Lisa with me to visit her family.

I took Lisa to her parents' house and had the privilege of eating dinner with them and getting to know the rest of the Will family. While I was there, I noticed that Anjy kept staring at her sister, unable to believe the miraculous transformation that had taken place in her life. I left to visit my parents, wondering what effect Lisa's witness would have on Anjy.

During her visit, Lisa realized that her room was full of various items that reminded her of her old life. To make a complete break with her past, she decided to destroy the remnants of her past life-style—especially her music. She asked her dad to join her in a backyard bonfire. He was elated! Anjy was amazed by the tremendous difference in her sister. She could not believe Lisa was getting rid of things she had once enjoyed, yet seemed so much happier without.

When I came back to pick up Lisa and return to Louisiana, I felt a tremendous burden for Anjy. I wanted to talk to her. While Lisa was getting ready to go, I said to her sister, "Could we go back to your room for a moment? I really need to talk to you."

"Sure," she said, leading me back to her bedroom, where we could talk without being heard.

"I'm going to tell you something, Anjy. I hope you don't mind my talking to you about this, but God has really put you on my heart this week. The Lord has shown me that you have gotten involved in something that is a lot bigger than you are. And it's a lot more dangerous than you even realize. What the Lord has shown me is that if you will do something about it now, it's not too late for you to be set free. He has given you an opportunity through what you've seen in Lisa's life to get out. I'm not saying you need to come to Louisiana, but I am making that opportunity available to you if you want to come. If you proceed down the path you're on, the devil is going to deceive you and drive you so deeply into it that it's going to become very difficult for you to turn around later on."

Anjy began to cry.

"I don't know what you've done," I said, "but there's not one thing you're involved in that the Lord can't get you out of. If you decide you want to come to Mercy Ministries, let me know."

As we parted, I said, "What's happened in Lisa's life is real."

"Oh, I know!" exclaimed Anjy through her tears. "I just can't believe what's happened to her. She's changed so much; it's just incredible!"

"Well, God is no respecter of persons," I said. "What He's done for her, He'll do for you; but it's your choice."

After tearful good-byes between Lisa and her family, we got in the car and drove to Monroe. I told Lisa about my conversation with her sister and she was overjoyed. We renewed our commitment to pray for Anjy.

About two weeks later Anjy called me. Weeping, she said, "I can't get what you told me off my mind. I know I need help. I want what happened to Lisa to happen to me."

"Are you saying you want to come down here?" I asked.

"Yeah."

"Well, that's no problem."

A few days later she arrived at our home for troubled girls and stayed seven months. With her, she brought some things that reminded her of the life she had been leading before. At Mercy Ministries, her life was transformed just like her sister's was. She decided to destroy the remnants of her old lifestyle too, so we got rid of all her occult paraphernalia on Halloween night. "How appropriate," I thought. "Just as Lisa had set a bad example before, now her good example led Anjy to commit her life to God!"

In December Lisa gave birth to a beautiful baby girl and chose to release her for adoption to a wonderful Christian family. After a month at home with her family, Lisa came back to Mercy Ministries to train to become a staff member. She had been given a spiritual burden for hurting girls.

The Widening Circle

As she worked with us, Lisa began to go to churches and youth groups with me to share her testimony and sing. She would challenge teens not to live a double standard but to commit their lives to God. To show them that living apart from God has horrible consequences, she did not hesitate to tell them about her own double standards and what had happened to her as a result. I was astounded at how bold she had become in sharing her testimony.

One time in New Orleans, a sixteen-year-old girl heard Lisa's testimony. She was pregnant and had been seriously considering having an abortion to erase her circumstances. Because of Lisa's willingness to share, that young woman was convicted and ended up going to the Mercy Ministries home for unwed mothers. Not only did she spare her child, but she became a committed Christian. The baby was joyfully adopted by a loving couple engaged in full-time ministry. It was wonderful to witness how God was using Lisa's past for His glory.

At the same time, David Will continued to tell the story of how he and his wife had "gained back two daughters from Satan and all of his destruction." As he ministered with the Imperials, he would give comfort to other parents with rebellious children. Between him and Lisa, a great many people have been touched and encouraged.

Because the Wills were so open about their family, I asked David to write a short article "From the Heart of a Father" for our newsletter, giving his perspective on what had happened to them. He was glad to do it, and I wrote an accompanying piece about Lisa and Anjy. We sent the copy to the printers, expecting to have a good newsletter to send to our supporters.

But God had much bigger plans.

The print shop misread the order and "accidentally" produced twenty-five thousand extra copies. Since they didn't have any use for them, the printers gave the newsletters to us. While we were wondering what to do with them, Armond and Bonnie told me they wanted to give them away at all the Imperials' concerts. We have received numerous phone calls from parents whose daughters needed our ministry and who heard about us from the Imperials. Without the help of the Wills and the other members of the Imperials, we would never have reached some of those desperate people.

My involvement with the Imperials eventually led to Lisa's and my going with them to minister in Germany. That was my first experience of speaking with an interpreter. Some German Christians still send us financial support. If it were not for God bringing Lisa and me together, I would never have had the opportunity to share about Mercy Ministries that far from home.

God also blessed Anjy in a very special way. After completing the program at Mercy Ministries, Anjy came home and enrolled in a two-year school of art. She has great talent, which her teachers observed, but she needed a job after finishing her training. In the summer of 1991, Kenneth Copeland Ministries published an article about the work of Mercy Ministries in its monthly publication. As a result of reading this article, one of the partners of Kenneth Copeland Ministries, Margaret Ellis, came to our Nashville office. She was so blessed by the article that she wanted more information about our homes. As it turned out, Margaret is a designer of fine jewelry. She mentioned to Lisa that she needed to train another designer, and Lisa told her about Anjy. Margaret interviewed and eventually hired Anjy first part-time, then full-time. God continues linking people together through the "ripple effect."

It occurred to me one day that the crisis pregnancy center that made Lisa change her mind about getting an abortion had played a major role in this course of events. At Mercy Ministries, we have the satisfying experience of following the girls' lives, and we often keep in touch with them long after they leave. But crisis pregnancy centers rarely receive that kind of encouragement. I wrote a letter to the center to tell the director how her work not only had saved the life of Lisa's baby, but had saved the lives of other babies and had led many young women to commit themselves to the Lord. It was wonderful to be able to share with other organizations how their efforts were also impacting lives.

Mercy Ministries is a ministry of multiplication. By restoring the broken lives of hurting girls and unwed mothers, we are given the opportunity to affect the lives of many others. The girls take what they have received and pass it on. Like Lisa, they become examples of how God "brought me up out of a horrible pit, out of the miry clay, and set my feet upon a rock and established my steps. He has put a new song in my mouth—praise to our God; many will see it and fear, and will trust in the LORD" (Ps. 40:2-3).

Because of the transparency of people like Lisa Will and others who have been a part of Mercy Ministries, lives are continuously being changed. When people who are hurting and are broken or in bondage see those who once walked on the ground where they now stand and have survived, they are eager to listen. If they can see the destruction of their sin and are willing to allow the love of God to penetrate their selfish ways, true healing can begin.

However, it takes the Lisa Wills of the world to boldly profess the Gospel of Jesus Christ and, in turn, spread the "ripple effect."

The Ripple Effect Continues

Lisa went on with her life and eventually met and married a special man. She has recently been reunited with the daughter she placed for adoption in 1989. The adoptive family even invited Lisa and her husband to spend a weekend with them —they had a wonderful time! Lisa works part-time for Mercy Ministries on occasion.

I mentioned earlier in the chapter that shortly after completing the Mercy program, Anjy went to work for an exclusive jewelry designer. She continues today with the same firm and has become a very successful designer in her own right. In 1997, she designed a special ring that has become the Mercy Ministries' graduation ring. Each ring is individually sized for each girl and Anjy handcrafts each piece for us.

Lisa and Anjy have a younger sister named Nicole. Even though Nicole never came to Mercy Ministries, she watched as both her sisters were transformed by going through the Mercy program. Interestingly enough, Nicole is the one who eventually became a full-time employee with Mercy Ministries in the year 2000 where she remains to this day. She has been valuable to us in her service for many years.

Lisa, Anjy, and Nicole's parents, David and Jan Will, continue to support the work of Mercy Ministries. As one of the original members of the Imperials, David still travels and shares their music ministry.

10

Against the Gates of Hell
The Purpose of the Church

But you are a chosen generation, a royal priesthood, a holy nation, His own special people, that you may proclaim the praises of Him who called you out of darkness into His marvelous light; who once were not a people but are now the people of God, who had not obtained mercy but now have obtained mercy. (1 Peter 2:9-10)

The smell almost knocked me over. As she came closer, I saw the filthiness of her clothes. Her hair was matted and looked as though there were bugs in it. I kept thinking that I did not want this girl to sit in my car. In that same moment, conviction gripped me. If this girl sensed my repulsion, we could lose her.

The police had phoned me at the home only minutes before to tell me Tammy's circumstances.

"I've never seen anything quite like it," the officer said with empathy in his voice. "If you can't help her, I don't know where she will end up."

I receive phone calls like this often. A parent, friend, neighbor, or counselor will call to tell me of a troubled girl they would like me to meet. So getting in my car and going out to bring this girl to Mercy Ministries was not unusual. I had made a commitment to the Lord when this ministry began that where He leads, I'll follow.

As I drove into the desolate area of the inner city, I recalled the details the officer had given: "We found her at this drug dealer's house we have been surveilling," he told me. "We advised her to get out now or she would probably end up in jail. Then we told her about you and Mercy Ministries, and she agreed to get help."

But now as I stood face-to-face with this seemingly hopeless transient, I saw how much unconditional love I lacked.

I hugged her quickly and tried not to gag from her smell. As we walked to the car, she turned toward me and softly spoke. "Ma'am, I don't think it is a good idea for me to get in your car," she said, obviously embarrassed.

"Don't worry about it, honey. You won't hurt anything," I tried to reassure her.

With pleading eyes she added, "Do you at least have something I can sit on?"

"Only this," I said and pulled an old jacket out of the trunk.

I crawled into the driver's seat and before we were a mile up the road, I felt myself becoming physically ill from the odor. But I couldn't show my disgust or this girl would think I was rejecting her. As if sensing my dilemma, she said, "I'm sorry I smell so bad. I can even smell myself."

"We'll get you cleaned up as soon as we get you home," I promised her.

Before we got there, I suggested we cut off the air and roll down the windows. Thankfully, she agreed.

Uneasiness swept over me. What if the girls don't receive her? What if they say something inappropriate and Tammy is destroyed? As I pulled in the driveway and got out of the car, the girls were waiting at the door. I had told them I was going to pick someone up, but I feared they would not be prepared for this. Thankfully the Holy Spirit had breathed upon their spirits. I love to watch Him work.

As Tammy took her first steps into Mercy Ministries, she was embraced by examples of unconditional love. For a

moment, she stood at the doorway, taking in the new surroundings. One by one the girls introduced themselves and
their compassion was evident.

Tammy again apologized for her odor. "I really am sorry I
smell this way," she whispered as she lowered her head.

Sensing her uneasiness, the girls took her hand and led her
down the hall.

As the voices trailed off and the girls disappeared into the
bathroom, I could hear them offering everything from towels and clothes to shampoo. The conviction I had felt earlier
swept over me again. I was supposed to be doing that. After
all, wasn't I the one who stood before congregations night
after night telling of the unconditional love we offer here?
But I had not even wanted this girl in my car. However, that
day, as I saw the love of God manifested in its purest form,
I realized that the message preached at Mercy Ministries
was working. Today it had preached to me.

As I lay in bed that night, the events of the day kept
replaying in my head. The girls had not hesitated to touch
Tammy's filthiness, and God has not hesitated to touch ours.
I realized the lesson the church of the Lord Jesus Christ,
especially myself, could learn from witnessing what I had
seen that day. If we, the church, could learn to love the
seemingly unlovable, our witness would be limitless.

I frequently travel to churches and Christian organizations to share the vision of the need to minister to hurting
girls and unwed mothers. Most of the people who hear me
speak become enthusiastic about responding to God's call.
Sometimes they commit to supporting Mercy Ministries
with their prayers. Sometimes they help Mercy Ministries
financially. Sometimes they catch the vision and begin to
implement it in their area. Whatever God leads them to do,
I am thankful most Christians who listen respond.

Most, but not all.

"I just don't think the church is responsible for those girls.

By having that home available, you are condoning premarital sex. We are simply to preach the Gospel."

I try to reply to such criticisms in a pleasant way. "Don't you think that the message might mean more if it is backed with actions? And isn't the message for those who are hurting, not for those who are well?" Unfortunately, I rarely receive a pleasant response: "I still don't believe the church can possibly care for all those disturbed girls, juvenile delinquents, and unwed mothers—they are the ones responsible for their situation. Besides, we pay taxes for the government to take care of them. Those girls need highly skilled, well-educated professionals. A bunch of Christians with good intentions can't possibly do much good."

No matter what I tell them about my own experience, some people have already made up their minds. They simply won't listen to the voice of reason, nor to the voice of God.

There are also many Christians who are aware of the mistreatment and abuse some girls suffer and who want very much to address the problem, but they are not sure what the solution is.

The solution is simple. It is the church. The people of God have the duty and privilege to bring restoration to broken lives.

It is up to us.

There is no one else.

The Mission of the Church

The church is called, as the people of God and the followers of Jesus Christ, to bring the message of salvation to those enslaved by sin. This mission means more than merely sharing a message, as important as that is. According to Scripture, the disciples were given broader instructions:

> And Jesus came and spoke to them, saying, "All authority has been given to Me in heaven and on earth. Go therefore and make disciples of all the nations, baptizing

them in the name of the Father and of the Son and of the Holy Spirit, teaching them to observe all things that I have commanded you; and lo, I am with you always, even to the end of the age." (Matthew 28:18-20)

The heart of the Great Commission is not just evangelism, but discipleship. While salvation from sin is an essential element of the Gospel, it also includes "teaching them to observe all things that I have commanded you" (Matt. 28:20). The Lord has not only charged His church with the task of planting seeds, He has given us the duty and privilege of being used by Him to make sure that what is planted grows to maturity and bears much fruit (see 1 Cor. 3:6-9). Just as Christians are called to apply the Gospel to their lives, they are called to teach others to do likewise. We have the responsibility to lay a foundation on which Godly lives can be built.

It is not enough, therefore, for the church only to preach a message, pass out tracts, or visit door-to-door to evangelize a neighborhood, though that may be the specific calling of some individual Christians. The church is commissioned to do works far surpassing these.

The church is called to do the work of Jesus. During Jesus' earthly ministry, He did more than preach a message; He reached out to a hurting and sinful people. In one of His first sermons, Jesus said He was sent not only "to preach the gospel to the poor," but "to heal the brokenhearted," and "to set at liberty those who are oppressed" (Luke 4:18).

And that is exactly what He did.

Jesus fed the hungry (see John 6:1-12) and gave drink to the thirsty (see John 2:1-10). He exalted the lowly (see Matthew 11:25). He consoled the mourning (see Luke 24:36). He forgave the criminal (see Luke 23:43). He released the captive (see Mark 5:1-20). He comforted the imprisoned (see Luke 4:18). He restored the fallen (see John 21:15-19). He fellowshipped with the outsider (see Luke 15:2). He suffered for the sake of His people (see Roman 5:8). He died for us (see Romans 4:25).

Not only does the Bible reveal that Jesus ministered to the needs of the people around Him, but it points out a special group to whom Christ especially ministered.

As Jesus was touring the countryside with His twelve apostles, proclaiming the Good News of the kingdom of Heaven, several women went along (see Luke 8:1-3). Until they met Jesus, these women had suffered from physical diseases and demonic possession. As a result of His work in their lives, not only were they restored, but they were privileged to proclaim the reality of Jesus Christ. One of them, Mary Magdalene, was honored by being the first to see and announce that Christ had risen (see John 20:11-18).

Scripture makes clear that Jesus was actively involved in ministering to people in need through works of compassion. It also makes clear that the hurt in the broken lives of women was close to His heart.

But that was only the beginning.

Jesus told the apostles that "he who believes in Me, the works that I do he will do also" (John 14:12). He commanded the church to follow the example of His ministry by not merely sharing a message of mercy, but by demonstrating mercy through their deeds.

And that is what they did.

In the New Testament, members of the church performed the same deeds as Christ. They fed the hungry and gave drink to the thirsty (see Acts 11:27-30). They exalted the lowly (see 1 Cor. 1:26-31). They consoled the mourning (see Acts 20:9-12). They forgave the criminal (see Acts 9:26-30). They released the captive (see Acts 16:16-18). They comforted the imprisoned (see Acts 16:25). They restored the fallen (see 2 Cor. 2:5-9). They fellowshipped with the outsider (see Acts 11:1-18). They suffered for the sake of God's people (see Col. 1:24).

The apostles reorganized the very structure of the early

church by adding new offices to sustain widows (see Acts 6:1-7). They understood that "pure and undefiled religion before God and the Father is this: to visit orphans and widows in their trouble, and to keep oneself unspotted from the world" (Jas. 1:27). Because of their experience in Godly living, the church gave these women a special teaching ministry (see 1 Tim. 5:9-10; Titus 2:3-5).

It is clear in Scripture that the church, from its conception, was actively involved in ministering to a hurting world. It is also plain that the broken lives of women were of special concern to these servants of Christ.

We who follow Jesus Christ and are part of His church are charged with continuing to carry out Christ's Great Commission in the midst of our present crisis. Not only must we share the Gospel with our words, but we must address with our actions the hurts and needs that confront us daily. We, not the government, are commanded to support the unwed mothers. We, not the government, are commanded to release the young women in bondage to drug addiction, promiscuity, and other sins. We, not the government, are commanded to bring young women into the embrace of eternal life. We, not the government, are commanded to bring restoration to broken lives. We, not the government, are commanded to be the hands, the feet, and the mouthpiece of Jesus Christ to the world of today.

It is up to us.

There is no one else.

The Power of God's People

Jesus did not merely give "marching orders" to the church. He did not tell His followers what to do and then leave them on their own to do it. The Great Commission involves much more than an assignment. The Gospel is not a "dead letter."

Jesus *empowered* His church to complete the mission He gave them. When He commanded the apostles to "make discipies of all the nations," He based His command on the fact that "All authority has been given to Me in heaven and on earth" (Matthew 28:18) and added the promise that "I am with you always, even to the end of the age" (Matthew 28:20). Therefore, just as Christ gave His Great Commission to the church and no one else, He also equipped the church and no one else to carry out His commission. Just as no other institution was appointed to "heal the brokenhearted," neither was any other institution equipped for such a healing work. Only the church has both the authority and the power to bring restoration to broken lives.

One of the many ways the Bible shows the incredible power of the church to bring restoration to broken lives is in the story of the woman who had the issue of blood for twelve years. According to Scripture, she "had suffered many things from many physicians. She had spent all that she had and was no better, but rather grew worse" (Mark 5:26). By merely touching Jesus' clothing, however, she was instantly healed.

While this story seems to refer only to a physical illness, at closer inspection we see it actually applies to *all* the effects of sin. Until Jesus came, an Israelite woman who had a blood disease was considered "unclean"—as if she had come in contact with death (see Lev. 15:25-33) or as if she were menstruating. She was not permitted to come near God's presence in the temple to worship. Anyone who touched her also became unclean for the rest of the day and was also prohibited from drawing near to God's presence. In fact, anyone who touched anything she contacted became unclean. In the Old Testament, the grave overpowered love. The unclean contaminated the clean. Judgment triumphed over mercy.

Death overcame life.

But Jesus transformed death into life.

Under the rules of the old creation, when the woman touched Jesus' clothes, He would have been made unclean. He would have been forced to go through a purification ritual. He would have been barred from drawing near to God's presence.

But He wasn't.

Jesus was not of the old creation. He was the beginning of the new creation (see 2 Cor. 5:17), the "firstborn from the dead" (Col. 1:18). Instead of becoming unclean, Jesus cleansed the woman. In Christ, love is stronger than the grave (see 1 Cor. 15:55-57). The clean cleanses the unclean (see 1 Tim. 4:3-5). "Mercy triumphs over judgment" (Jas. 2:13).

Life overcomes death.

At Mercy Ministries, a multitude of girls have been through many secular treatment programs and have experienced the best the government rehabilitation systems and the recovery industry offer. Some were the victims of others' sin. Some were the slaves of their own sin. These girls were in bondage to sin and death. And, after all the secular treatment they received, their problems seemed to become worse.

But Jesus transformed death into life.

Although Jesus Christ has ascended into heaven, His cleansing, resurrecting touch is still available to anyone who is willing to reach out. Despite the fact that He is sitting at the right hand of God the Father, His purpose is to intercede for us so that we can be free from the sins that bind us.

Just as Jesus was anointed by the Holy Spirit at the beginning of His ministry (see Mark 1:10), the church received the Holy Spirit at the beginning of its ministry (see Acts 2:4). Through the Holy Spirit, the church has the power to accomplish the mission He gave us (see Luke 24:49). Only the church has the power of the Holy Spirit. Only the church is "the pillar and ground of the truth" (1 Tim. 3:15 NKJV). Only the church is able to attack the gates of hell (see Matt. 16:18).

Never Give Up

When Rhonda came to Mercy Ministries, she suffered from an eating disorder, substance abuse, and lesbianism. She had been both physically and sexually abused while she was growing up. In addition, Rhonda had gone to a dozen secular treatment programs that had not helped her.

I looked at the hard, bitter expression chiseled into her face and thought, "There's just no way. We've helped lots of girls in the past, and their lives have been totally transformed, but this one is a wall of stone. There's just no way." I was almost tempted to contact a private secular counselor—perhaps someone with a Ph.D. from a prestigious school. But deep down I knew that would not solve the real problem.

Instead, I prayed for a miracle.

Christians commonly doubt that they can minister to the needs of hurting people without a college degree in psychology. Even leaders of the church become intimidated by the wisdom of the world. Perhaps if I had not witnessed how powerless the secular treatment programs seem to be to bring about restoration, I would be intimidated as well. But I have learned from experience that book knowledge will never reach girls like Rhonda. Girls like this can only be truly helped *by encountering God Himself.* When God led His people out of Egypt, He commanded them to conquer the land of Canaan and promised He would be their strong tower. But when the people saw the enemy facing them, they lost faith in God. They complained that "we were like grasshoppers in our own sight" in comparison to the inhabitants of Canaan (Num. 13:33). As a result of their lack of faith, the Israelites were forced to wander in the wilderness between Egypt and Canaan for forty years (see Num. 14:34).

Like the Israelites, we often question our ability to follow through with the Great Commission. We often walk by sight, not by faith (see 2 Cor. 5:7). We often appear "like grasshoppers in our own sight."

It is all too easy to view ourselves from this natural viewpoint.

As we look at the rising number of abortions, the increasing number of illegitimate babies, the expanding problem of drug abuse, and a host of other woes affecting young women and others, it is tempting to give up. But we must resist the temptation and trust in God. If we give in to our doubts and don't believe God's promises to empower us and provide for us, we lack power and provision (see Jas. 1:6-7). If we believe we are incapable of ministering to the severe needs of people abused and enslaved in sin, then we will not be able to help them.

The church does not appear capable of bringing restoration to broken lives. But that should not surprise us. Jesus prefers to work through people who are humanly incapable of accomplishing His will:

> Brothers, think of what you were when you were called. Not many of you were wise by human standards; not many were influential; not many were of noble birth. But God chose the foolish things of the world to shame the wise; God chose the weak things of the world to shame the strong. He chose the lowly things of this world and the despised things—and the things that are not—to nullify the things that are, so that no one may boast before him. (1 Corinthians 1:26-29 NIV)

Despite our limitations, we "can do all things through Christ who strengthens us" (Phil. 4:13). As Paul wrote, "We are more than conquerors through Him who loved us" (Rom. 8:37). We don't need to fear anyone in the world, because He that is in us is greater than he who is in the world (see 1 John 4:4). We need not fear, because Jesus has overcome the world (see John 16:33).

By working through His church, Christ performs two miracles. First, He changes the hearts of hurting people and gives them new lives. In return, they become new creatures. Secondly, He uses us to do it.

When Rhonda left the home, not only was her heart transformed but her appearance had been changed. Not because of any great work of the staff of Mercy Ministries, but because of a miracle worked by the Holy Spirit in her life, Rhonda now displayed a countenance of one who had encountered divine mercy. No longer was her face cold and hard; it was warm and inviting. In Christ, Rhonda had been transformed. Her bitterness was replaced with forgiveness. Her physical appearance was indicative of a changed heart—change that caused her beauty to start on the inside and be reflected on the outside.

I hope and pray that Rhonda and the other girls who have gone through one of the Mercy Ministries homes are the first-fruits of much more to come. If the Holy Spirit can use the church to bring restoration to the broken lives of those young women, we know He can do the same for other young women as more homes are started across the country.

The only thing necessary is that God's people hear His call and believe His promises. Only then will we be able to bring restoration to broken lives.

It is up to us.

There is no one else.

A Strategy of Submission

Many Christians are surprised to discover that I have not only spoken to and raised support from non-Christian groups, but I have even been invited to speak in public schools. When people—even non-Christians—learn of Mercy Ministries' desire to help troubled girls and unwed mothers, they are moved by God to respond favorably. As a result, I have been given many opportunities to share the Gospel in places only God could make available.

As many Christians have come to realize the full scope of the Gospel, they have begun to try to positively influence the world. There is nothing wrong with this. Abortion is an example of an issue Christians need to address. The murder of unborn babies is hateful in God's sight and should be illegal. It is right for Christians to fight against such evil.

But if Christians oppose abortion exclusively through confrontational demonstrations and political lobbying, it is not likely that we will succeed in stopping it; nor are we likely to give the world a true picture of Christ's love. While these activities may be justified and necessary, the church also needs to provide an alternative for the unwed mothers who are enticed to abort their children.

Most of those who are having abortions are not politicians; they are frightened young women, many of whom do not have the money or the courage to bring a living baby into the world alone. Furthermore, they are the people who, if they do not feel the healing love and mercy of Christ, will likely fall more deeply into sin—including having more abortions—to cover the guilt, anger, fear, and hurt of previous transgressions and circumstances.

By meeting the needs of unwed mothers, the church has its best opportunity to bring an end to the abortion holocaust. By acting as feeling, caring disciples of Christ, we are able to cut to the heart of the problem. The process may seem slow, but it is thorough and will ripple, spreading Christ to others.

The reason we offer young women an alternative to abortion is not simply because it will become easier to persuade them to choose life—though that is true. As an example of the church engaged in active service, we will cause the world to respect and listen to what Christians have to say. In other words, what they see us *do* will speak much louder than what they hear us *say*. As Jesus said, "Let your light so shine before men, that they may see your good works and glorify your Father in heaven" (Matt. 5:16).

Jesus made clear that in order to reach positions of leadership, Christians must be willing to serve.

> You know that the rulers of the Gentiles lord it over them, and those who are great exercise authority over them. Yet it shall not be so among you; but whoever

desires to become great among you, let him be your servant. And whoever desires to be first among you, let him be your slave—just as the Son of Man did not come to be served, but to serve, and to give His life a ransom for many. (Matthew 20:25-28)

Throughout the Bible, positions of leadership are given to those who humble themselves and serve others.

Jacob was a servant. For seven years he slaved for his uncle Laban to marry Laban's younger daughter, Rachel. But he was tricked into receiving the older daughter, Leah. Instead of giving up, he worked seven years longer. Despite the fact that Laban kept changing his wages and consumed his daughters' inheritance, eventually Jacob was immensely blessed by God with a great family and great wealth. Jacob's service brought him prosperity (see Gen. 29—31).

Joseph was a servant. After being sold into slavery by his brothers, Joseph served in the house of an Egyptian official. Despite his faithfulness and diligence, he was falsely accused and thrown into prison. He continued to faithfully serve in prison, and God exalted him to the right hand of Pharaoh, king of Egypt, where he ruled the civilized world of that time. As a result, Joseph was able to extend mercy to his brothers and save his family from starvation. Joseph's service brought him authority (see Gen. 37—47).

David was a servant. The youngest of his brothers, David served his father as a shepherd and a messenger. Later, he served Saul as a musician and a soldier. Instead of attaining honor, however, David became a fugitive who had to constantly flee for his life. Eventually God vindicated David and gave him a throne over all of Israel. As a result, David was able to show mercy to Saul's household. David's service brought him a crown (see 1 Sam. 16—2 Sam. 9).

Esther was a servant. In making herself beautiful to win the heart of the king, Esther submitted to the advice of the king's servants. She was crowned queen of the empire. When her cousin and foster-parent, Mordecai, told her to reveal to the king who she was, Esther again submitted—though it meant risking her life. She even served the enemy of God's people a banquet. As a result, her requests on behalf of the people of God were granted, and she was restored to the king's favor. Esther's service brought the salvation of her people (see Est. 1—10).

Nehemiah was a servant. As the king's cupbearer, Nehemiah served the Persian emperor by protecting him from being poisoned. When he was given authority to rebuild the walls of Jerusalem, he did not "lord it over" the Jews. Instead of taxing them to support himself as he had every right to do, Nehemiah supported himself as well as many others. Not only did he oversee the rebuilding of the walls, but he took part in the physical labor. As a result, Jerusalem was a restored city and the Jews were restored to God's favor. Nehemiah's service brought him a city (see Neh. 1—13).

Jesus was a servant. Although He had every right to be equal with the Father, Jesus humbled Himself. He served His disciples by washing their feet and giving them food and drink. Though He was innocent, He submitted to dying like a common criminal. Because of His humble service, God exalted Jesus to sit enthroned in heaven. Jesus' service brought Him the kingdom of God.

These are a few of the many biblical figures who were given authority and influence because of their service. If we desire for God to give us favor in the eyes of men, we should follow these examples.

We must humble ourselves and serve others as Christ humbled Himself and served us. We must meet the needs of others before trying to bring restoration to their lives.

It is up to us.

There is no one else.

11

To the End of the Earth
The Future of Mercy Ministries

Have I not commanded you? Be strong and of good courage; do not be afraid, nor be dismayed, for the LORD your God is with you wherever you go. (Joshua 1:9)

In April 1989, I received a phone call from Pastor L. H. Hardwick of Christ Church in Nashville. I had attended his church on Sunday nights when I lived there in the late 1970s. He asked if I remembered him.

"Of course, I remember you," I assured him.

"Well, we've heard about your work in Louisiana, and we've been trying to figure out what we can do that will be a positive response to the abortion issue. We wondered if you'd come and speak to us about what you're doing in Louisiana."

That phone call would prove to be very significant. Since both homes had been operating smoothly for some time, I had begun to have a new vision of where Mercy Ministries was supposed to go. For years I had assumed I was called to operate the two homes in Monroe. Now I began to think that Mercy Ministries should build and run more homes across the nation. The only question was where to build the first new home. Nashville occasionally crossed my mind, but I thought it was because I was a bit homesick. I prayed regularly for the Lord's direction and waited for His guidance.

When Pastor Hardwick first called me to come speak about my work, it didn't occur to me that the Lord was answering my prayer by leading me back to my home state. I went to Nashville and gave a presentation about Mercy Ministries to a group of community leaders and others interested in starting an adoption agency. That night, as I showed slides depicting various activities at the home, as well as many pictures of babies saved from abortion, their hearts were stirred. They realized through what I shared that the greatest need is for the young girls in trouble to have a place to live and come to know Christ, not an adoption agency. The adoption agency would come later as a result of first reaching out to the girls.

By the time I had been to Nashville three times at Pastor Hardwick's invitation, I realized the Holy Spirit was moving on my heart to locate there and establish a large facility for unwed mothers. Since I had lived in Nashville years earlier when I worked for the state and for Teen Challenge, I still knew many people there who supported me for many years. Most importantly, however, was the immense support and encouragement that Pastor Hardwick gave me.

In the fall of 1989, while I was still praying about the possibility of establishing a home in Nashville, Pastor Hardwick cleared two weeks off of his calendar to introduce me to key people in the Nashville area. This was a big sacrifice for him to make since Christ Church is quite large and demands much of his time. Nevertheless, he, his wife, and I met with forty pastors from different denominations so I could present the vision of Mercy Ministries and explain that we wanted to establish a home for unwed mothers in the Nashville area. Their response was favorable, and I saw it as further confirmation that God was leading me to Nashville.

When it was time to make the move, I asked Lisa Will to return to Nashville with me to be on staff. She welcomed the opportunity to be close to her family again, but she also welcomed the opportunity to share her testimony in the same place where Satan had tried to destroy her. We immediately began meeting needs in the area by counseling troubled girls and unwed mothers, although there was no home for them. We were overwhelmed with calls from hurting girls and families, but we continued to provide counseling and ministry at no cost. Before opening our Tennessee home, we directed more than sixty girls to our homes in Louisiana—which further demonstrated the need for a facility in Nashville.

The Call Continues

In Nashville, God immediately began blessing us with the support of many Christians and churches. Because of Pastor Hardwick's commitment to Mercy Ministries, he scheduled me to share the vision at a Sunday night service soon after I moved.

Before I was able to speak, however. Pastor Hardwick came to me with tears in his eyes. "Nancy," he said, "God has convicted me that you need to speak in both Sunday morning services, and not on Sunday night. I believe that all the people in the church need to hear what you have to say and need to have an opportunity to get involved. It has to be on Sunday morning so everyone will hear the message."

Tears came to my eyes when I realized how generous this was of Pastor Hardwick. Over four thousand people attend Christ Church each Sunday. Not many pastors would give up the pulpit and allow someone else to have their Sunday morning time.

Those Sunday services were a special time as God ministered to others and moved the hearts of many to provide support for Mercy Ministries. I was so grateful that Pastor Hardwick had invited me to use the worship service to proclaim God's message of mercy.

The Lord touched the hearts of many in the congregation as I spoke of the multitude of troubled girls and unwed mothers we had helped. Some were brought to tears as I told them of the hurting, broken lives that still needed to be restored through the power of the Gospel. After I finished my message, Pastor Hardwick stood up and unexpectedly received an offering for Mercy Ministries. Despite the fact that an offering had already been taken for the church, the congregation gave almost twenty thousand dollars to help the work in Nashville begin.

More important than any money collected, however, were the many women who responded to Pastor Hardwick's altar call.

While showing the slides which contrasted graphic photographs of aborted babies with the beautiful portraits of adopted children, I said, "Statistically speaking, one out of every four women in America today has had an abortion. If you are one of these, I want you to know that I am not showing these slides to condemn you in any way, because if you have asked God to forgive you, then it is under the blood of Jesus and you are no longer guilty. But if you haven't asked Him to, there's forgiveness with God and you can receive it today.

"I'm showing these slides because God has dealt with me to expose the lies of the abortion industry, who print in their literature that the unborn baby is just a little blob of tissue and that having an abortion is like getting a wart removed. I do this in hope of preventing future abortions. In no way is this meant to condemn you. In fact, Jesus wants to heal you if you still hurt over that."

After I finished speaking and we received the offering for Mercy Ministries, Pastor Hardwick dismissed the congregation but said, "If there are people with needs and you would like prayer in any of the areas Nancy mentioned, please come forward."

In response to the invitation, the front of the church was flooded with women who were crying and sobbing. They told me the traumas of their past abortions which they had never really dealt with. They wanted release from the pain and guilt they were suffering. Many of these women also testified that, despite their mistake, the Lord had blessed them with a husband and children. Yet they had never confessed their past sin to God or received His forgiveness. They were thankful that God had brought to the surface the guilt they had been suppressing so they could deal with it.

Additionally, several parents came forward, asking for prayer for their daughters. Soon afterward, some of these girls went to the homes in Louisiana. These parents were grateful that God had worked to let them know about Mercy Ministries in their time of need. They hadn't known where to turn.

Besides that Sunday service, there were many other ways God blessed me and demonstrated that He wanted a new home built in Nashville. The way He provided Mercy Ministries with property was a special blessing.

For a long time, we prayed and searched for an appropriate piece of property where we could build a home. We looked everywhere we could think to look, especially out in the country where we had hoped to find something inexpensive. Nothing turned up. The zoning board limited our options by ruling that we would have to buy property in a commercial area for them to consider zoning us.

In November, the realtor finally called. "I've found the perfect piece of property!"

"Well, where is it?" I asked.

"It's right next door to Christ Church."

"Are you kidding me?" We had been looking all around the Nashville area for a place, and God had chosen one right next to a supportive church. I had never noticed it before.

We settled on a reasonable price for the property and signed a purchase agreement contingent on approval by the zoning board. I began to pray that God would provide us the money to buy the land.

Because of the generous contributions from several well-known national ministries and the sacrificial gifts the Lord moved individuals to make, we were able to acquire the property. From December of 1990 until the following June we waited for zoning approval. We had a public meeting with the people who lived in the area to let them know what we were going to do with the property, and they had no objections. We were later granted permission by the Metro Zoning Board to build as many as five buildings on the land.

During that time, we began raising money to build the home debt-free. We installed water and sewer lines on the property at the cost of twenty-two thousand dollars. God blessed us with the money to pay cash for this work.

The Lord has continued to confirm His call to me in Nashville by bringing co-laborers to help in the Nashville office. In answer to a real need through continual prayer, one special person was brought to Mercy Ministries to take over the administrative and business hassles, allowing me to spend more time helping girls and speaking to Christians across the country.

When we decided it was time to hold a "Celebration of Life" banquet, I realized we needed someone who knew how to organize it. Judy Wilson, my secretary at the time, mentioned Linda Hilliard, who helped with the administrative affairs of the Christ Church Choir.

"Call her," I said, "and ask if she would be willing to help us. If not, see if she can at least serve as a consultant. I don't want her to feel pressured." I didn't know Linda very well, and I wasn't sure what she would say.

Judy called her, and without hesitation Linda volunteered to take charge of the banquet herself and recruited others to help. As I observed Linda's capabilities, I was extremely impressed with both her efficiency and her desire to help. I knew God was going to use her to help with Mercy Ministries. I had been praying for someone with a heart for God who also had business skills and the ability to work with people. This would give me more time to spend on other aspects of ministry, and Linda was exactly the type of person I had been praying for. As soon as I felt the timing was right, I asked if she was interested in working with us. She told me she and her husband, Wayne, would pray about it. I later learned that Linda had twenty years of experience in ministry, including five years working for Dina Kartsonakis—the contemporary Christian pianist—and two years for interior designer Landy Gardner, who is also the director of the Christ Church Choir. She had experience in Christian publishing and television as well.

In November 1991 God worked everything out for Linda to leave her former job and work for Mercy Ministries full-time as Executive Director. She did an incredible job keeping the ministry going and being a strong support for me. Her continual productivity was a daily reminder to me of how faithful God is to bring the right people to get the job done.

The banquet was a great success, thanks to Linda's work and to many volunteers who helped. The Imperials were there to support us, and they sang the national anthem to open the evening. David and Lisa Will told about how their family had been blessed by Mercy Ministries, where Lisa and Anjy had turned for help. Joe Rodgers, ambassador to France during the Reagan administration, acted as our master of ceremonies. The former Tennessee Secretary of State, Bryant Millsaps, spoke out against abortion in support of our work. Our keynote speaker was Cal Thomas. He delivered a speech on behalf of Mercy Ministries that was clever and convicting, humorous and humbling. "Good evening my fellow products of conception and former fetuses," he began, stirring up loud laughter.

As Cal continued, he addressed America's wavering mentality. "This is a war we are in, in case you haven't noticed. You can't be of no opinion in this war, because if you're not serving on one side you're serving on the other.

"One day when those of us who have accepted Him are finally with Him in heaven, somebody's going to come up and introduce themselves and say, 'Do you see that woman over there?'

" 'Yeah.'"

" 'That's my mother, and I thought you might like to know that what you did that night in Nashville, in 1991, caused my mother to call this phone number. She was scheduled for an abortion. She talked to one of the counselors at Mercy Ministries and they convinced her not to have an abortion, and because of that I had a chance to get to know Jesus Christ as my personal Savior and I just wanted to say thank you.' "

Things were silent as Cal closed. "Everything that Mercy Ministries is involved in is free. You can't get a free abortion. They make a lot of money killing babies. This is big business. God only has you.

"How much is a human life worth?" he asked.

It was a good question.

Celebration of Life

In an attempt to unite the body of Christ against abortion and in favor of promoting life, Mercy Ministries began holding "Celebration of Life" rallies. These rallies are designed to reach different areas around the country, to break down denominational walls, and to communicate with Christians from all walks of life. We speak about abortion, challenging the church to work together to present positive solutions to the problems we face. We tell them about the work of Mercy Ministries and offer them an opportunity to participate in it through financial contributions, volunteer service, and intercessory prayer.

God brought several Christian artists to work with me at these events. The contemporary Christian group, the Imperials, appeared in concert at several "Celebration of Life" rallies. Point of Grace, Naomi Judd and other artists have volunteered their time and talents as well.

Another group of Christians that helps Mercy Ministries in its outreach to the church is the adoptive parents of the babies who are saved from abortion. Many of these couples have moving testimonies, which they share at the rallies. For example, one woman went through twelve corrective surgeries and still was not able to have children. She and her husband have since been blessed with two beautiful boys from Mercy Ministries.

In another case, a young woman who had always wanted to have children had to have a hysterectomy when she was twenty-six. She was crushed at the thought that she would never be able to have children. She eventually met a man, and they fell in love and were married. He, too, wanted to have children, so they prayed about adopting. Through Mercy Ministries, God has given them the child they have always wanted.

Pastor Perry and Sue Gaspard at Abundant Life, a large church in Lake Charles, Louisiana, wanted desperately to have a child, but after many years of marriage had been unable to do so. They considered adoption, but Perry wanted to be in God's will and he was uncertain whether a child of no blood relation would fit into their family. God brought along a beautiful young lady, however, who had almost aborted her child but, because of her mother's prayers, chose to go to the Mercy Ministries home. Like the Gaspards, this young lady was very cautious about adoption and was very concerned that her baby be placed with the right family.

This young birth mother made a long list of what she wanted in the couple who would raise her child; this lengthy catalog of qualifications fit Perry and Sue exactly. They received their beautiful baby girl when she was only three days old. The birth mother has gone on with her life and is doing wonderfully. Now Perry and Sue's daughter is the joy of their lives!

Our relationship with Perry and Sue opened the door for us to have a "Celebration of Life" rally at Abundant Life, and they continue to be strong supporters of Mercy Ministries.

The other testimonies of adoptive parents who appear at Point of Grace concerts and other events are especially touching when they show off their beautiful children. One proud father spoke at the rally while holding his precious son, whom he had adopted from Mercy Ministries. This daddy was beaming with pride as he stood next to his wife and told the crowd how much their son meant to them.

"It sure is a joy to be here with these other families," he said, gesturing to the other parents on stage with their children. "I can't tell you what it does to me to look at them—it's absolutely wonderful!"

Then he shifted his attention to his son. "But this little live wire here has just been a blessing to us to no end. We received Jack from Mercy Ministries on our fifteenth wedding anniversary. We were transformed at that time from being a happy couple to a family." His voice was choked with emotion.

"You know," he went on, still beaming, "we're to judge trees by their fruit. Well, we're holding some fruit here and it's good fruit."

The stories of parents are especially moving when we show the slides that portray the awful consequences of abortion, and what could have been had those girls not had a place to go. As another adoptive father said while addressing the audience: "When you see the photos up here of the abortions, your heart just *breaks*—especially when you look down and look at something like this." He nodded to the tiny baby cradled in his arms.

"For my wife and me this has been a great joy in our life. We spent the first seven—" He swallowed hard to fight back joyful tears—"seventeen years without someone. This child has really been a blessing."

The parents and their children show what can happen when the church comes together and promotes life instead of abortion. I am grateful for their willingness to share their moving testimonies with the people who attend the rallies.

With the help of the Christian artists and the adoptive parents, Mercy Ministries is able to present a convincing case to the people of God that the church must stand united against abortion by offering young women a viable alternative. Not only will such a stance save the lives of children and lead to the transformations of young women, it will also cause the world to respect the church for doing something positive that will bring unspeakable joy to the lives of countless numbers of people.

These rallies have an impact on the lives of Christians, not just to get them excited to join together to save the lives of children, but also to minister healing and forgiveness to those women who have had abortions. Tragically, many women in the church have fallen into sin, and like King David (see 2 Samuel 11), have attempted to hide it through the death of an innocent person. Instead of being forever enslaved to guilt for what they have done, like King David they need to experience God's cleansing forgiveness (see Psalm 51). These women need to be assured that they can be restored through Jesus Christ. Many times the altars are filled with women who need prayer to be released from the pain and grief of past abortions.

After one of our "Celebration of Life" rallies in Nashville, David Will and his family were eating at a restaurant. A woman at the restaurant who had heard David and Lisa tell what happened in their family sent them an anonymous note on a napkin:

> I don't want to approach you. I was at the benefit for Mercy Ministries and was very blessed by the concert. I enjoyed it very much. Four years ago I was in a crisis pregnancy with nowhere to turn. The pressure to choose abortion was very great. I could not find the courage to tell my family and I was not married. I went to a clinic of Planned Parenthood. They said abortion was the solution. However, they did not tell me the kind of hell I would live in because of my choice. I am a Christian

and was a Christian at the time I made that choice. It has taken me a long time to forgive and let go. In the past six months God has healed me from those scars. He's still healing me today. Your ministry is a wonderful outreach to a hurting world. I appreciate what you do. In His name. God bless you. Thanks!

I feel a special burden for women like this. A great many of those who end up in our homes for troubled girls are there because they cannot handle the guilt of one or more past abortions. These girls often come from Christian homes. Instead of allowing them to fall away, we need to extend mercy to them and pull them back into the body of Christ.

Ever Onward

At first I assumed all God wanted me to do was start the homes in Louisiana. Undoubtedly, the Lord did not want me to start planning anything else until I had completed those two homes and operated them for a while. At the time, that alone seemed like an incredibly difficult task. If I had known I was supposed to establish more homes in other parts of the country, I might have been overwhelmed. God worked in my life so that I took one step at a time.

Eventually, however, I realized that the two homes in Louisiana were not enough to care for all the troubled girls and unwed mothers who were applying from all across the country. More homes were needed. As a result of the Lord's guidance, a great deal of effort, and many mistakes, Mercy Ministries now had working models of a home for troubled girls and a home for unwed mothers. We had even compiled a manual on "How to Establish a Girls' Home." The manual made the task of building more homes more feasible, and it helped in training new staff. God was calling us to reproduce the Louisiana homes in other places across the nation.

I especially started thinking about establishing more

maternity homes. I have become more and more convinced that the Supreme Court will eventually overturn *Roe v. Wade*. When that happens, it will become absolutely necessary to have more places where unwed mothers can be cared for and counseled from the Word of God. Until then, more young women will be seeking alternatives to abortion as other states follow the lead of Pennsylvania by requiring that fetal development be explained to women and that minors have parental consent. We must be ready to open our hearts and our homes.

Pressing On

Christian life is not to be lived by resting on past accomplishments. Rather we are called to follow the example of the apostle Paul, who didn't base his confidence on any of his past achievements, but stated:

> Not that I have already attained, or am already perfected; but I press on, that I may lay hold of that for which Christ Jesus has also laid hold of me. Brethren, I do not count myself to have apprehended; but one thing I do, forgetting those things which are behind and reaching forward to those things which are ahead, I press toward the goal for the prize of the upward call of God in Christ Jesus. (Philippians 3:12-14)

I frequently tell the young women who come to Mercy Ministries that they must not dwell on the past but firmly face the future in newness of life. How can I not take my own advice? Although we are very thankful to God for what He has done in the past, there is much more to be done. Like all Christians and—hopefully—*with* all Christians, we must continue to strive toward "the upward call" God has commanded us to complete, "forgetting those things which are behind and reaching forward to those things which are ahead."

While in the Old Testament God told Israel to merely take the land of Canaan (see Josh. 1:1-9), in the New Testament

Jesus commanded His church to go out into all the earth (see Matt. 28:18-20). With the power of the Holy Spirit at our disposal, there is no reason for Christians to be content with limited ministry. God wants us to bring restoration to every area of the world, including the broken lives of troubled girls and unwed mothers. With Jesus' promise to be with us "to the end of the age," there is no reason for Christians to be intimidated by the seeming impossibility of any task He has given us to do. God wants us to accomplish great things for Him, including starting homes for girls across the country, where lives that have almost been destroyed by the forces of hell are healed by God's love and power.

We must follow the "upward call." For many, it will mean the difference between life and death.

For Such a Time as This

We live in hard times.

The church faces an onslaught of broken homes, abused and abandoned children, juvenile delinquents, teenage alcohol abusers and drug users, unwed mothers, and aborted babies. Too often the church has failed to respond to this present crisis. We Christians have prayed and studied the Bible—and this is essential. *However*, the most important aspect of our Christian life is to win the lost. We must reach hurting people with the Gospel in their time of need, rather than sending them off to secular and state programs that, at best, provide only temporary relief.

We live in hard times, but Esther also lived in hard times. The Jews were an ethnic minority scattered throughout a pagan empire. Worse, they were all—man, woman, and child—condemned to death by the decree of the king. When Esther's cousin Mordecai asked her to use her position as queen to intercede on behalf of the Jews, she at first refused. To go into the presence of the king uninvited was a capital crime unless he decided to make an exception. Since the king had not seen Esther for a month, she doubted that she would find favor with him.

Mordecai exhorted her to save her people, telling her: "Yet who knows whether you have come to the kingdom for such a time as this?" (Est. 4:14).

Esther had to help the people of God. She commanded all the Jews to fast for three days, but she did not stop there. She completed her fast by taking direct action and risked her life by entering the king's presence. As a result, not only were the lives of the Jews saved and their enemies destroyed, but people were converted in a massive revival that spanned the entire empire (see Est. 8:17).

It is my conviction that Mercy Ministries of America has-been raised up in the kingdom "for such a time as this."

One time I was studying what the Bible teaches about fasting. I discovered that the fast Jesus wants us to hold is not what we usually think of as a fast. It is my hope that we as the church will take action and bring forth what is described in Isaiah 58:

Is this not the fast I have chosen:
To loose the bonds of wickedness,
To undo the heavy burdens,
To let the oppressed go free,
And that you break every yoke?

Is it not to share your bread with the hungry,
And that you bring to your house the poor who are cast out;
When you see the naked, that you cover him,
And not hide yourself from your own flesh?

Then your light shall break forth like the morning,
Your healing shall spring forth speedily,
And your righteousness shall go before you;
The glory of the LORD shall be your rear guard.

Then you shall call, and the LORD will answer;
You shall cry, and He will say, "Here I am."
If you take away the yoke from your midst,
The pointing of the finger, and speaking wickedness.

If you extend your soul to the hungry
And satisfy the afflicted soul,
Then your light shall dawn in the darkness,
And your darkness shall be as the noonday.

The LORD will guide you continually,
And satisfy your soul in drought,
And strengthen your bones;
You shall be like a watered garden,
And like a spring of water, whose waters do not fail.

Those from among you
Shall build the old waste places;
You shall raise up the foundations of many generations;
And you shall be called the Repairer of the Breach,
The Restorer of the Streets to Dwell In. (Isaiah 58:6-12)

The Scripture is clear: If we wish to see our churches and ministries restored to the place they once had in our nation, we must lead broken lives to Christ. If we desire for people to respect the church, we must "preach the gospel to the poor" and "heal the brokenhearted." If we want God to prosper us in our endeavors, we must proclaim "deliverance to the captives and recovery of sight to the blind," and "set at liberty those who are oppressed" (Luke 4:18).

As I have often said, Mercy Ministries is not just an outreach to troubled girls or unwed mothers; it is a ministry to the church of Jesus Christ. I hope and pray that it will be used by God to call Christians to do what we are supposed to do — and to be what we are supposed to be.

If we humbly obey God's mandate of mercy by meeting the needs of troubled girls and unwed mothers and attempt to bring restoration to broken lives. God will bless us more than we can ever imagine. He is capable of giving the church favor in the eyes of men. He is capable of turning the hearts of our leaders so that they may make laws against abortion and other evils. He is capable of bringing repentance and restoration to the entire nation. He will do all this and more, if we will remain faithful to Him.

If we keep the fast He has chosen.

Perhaps the Lord has blessed you in order to give you the privilege of taking part in His work.

Perhaps you have come to the kingdom for such a time as this.

12

---

16 Years Later

16 Years Later....

I finished writing all the previous chapters in 1992, and it is now 2008. I am amazed at all God has done since that time. First of all, let me update you about what has happened with the Nashville home. I brought you to the point where we had actually bought the property and were raising the money and believing to build debt-free. Let me tell you what has happened after that time.

Nashville Home Completed Debt-Free

We continued believing God for the money to build the home in Nashville, and He continued to touch people's hearts to help. Only a few months passed before we were able to pay off the property note. That was a very special time!

I spoke in the Sunday morning service at Christ Church in Nashville, and Pastor Hardwick and I had the privilege of striking a match to the property note and burning it in front of the whole congregation to let everyone know that this debt was paid! That was probably one of the most enjoyable experiences of my life, as the crowd exploded with cheers.

Then the next challenge came—believing for the money to build the home debt-free. We didn't know how God was going to do it, but we knew it was going to happen! We had the plans drawn up and an artist rendering of the 20,000 square foot, 40-bed facility, and we continued to tell people that we were going to build it debt-free. I knew in my heart that when we reached the half-way mark of the actual cost that we would start the building process and we would let people know that we were paying for it as we built it. We felt that this would be a motivating factor for people to continue to pray and to believe with us and also to give toward the project.

Many people began to give as we continued speaking out the vision every opportunity we had. We had a dinner under a tent on the property, and there were over 1,000 people in attendance. Many hearts were touched that night to give, and it was a real boost to our overall goal.

In 1993, we had enough money to actually break ground. We had a ground-breaking ceremony which was covered by our local news affiliates. Shortly after that construction began, and it was so exciting to see the work actually happening. Around this same time, I was invited to speak on a national television program. They wanted me to share about the fact that we were building a home debt-free, paying for it as we go. They asked me to give an update about where we were with our finances and to share why were building it and to tell about some of the changed lives that had occurred through Mercy Ministries. I actually showed footage of construction going up, and spoke the vision into the television cameras that aired throughout the country. They gave our contact details and it wasn't long until many people from all over the United States began sending in contributions.

One such gift came from a very unlikely source—let me explain. A woman in Texas whom I had never met wrote me a brief note and enclosed a check for $100,000. It turns out that she saw the program that night, and made a decision to give this amount in memory of her son, Stevie Ray Vaughan, one of the world's most influential blues guitarists. Her son had gone through troubled times in his own life and had become a Christian, and she knew that this was something that he would definitely want to support if he was alive. That particular gift was a huge help as it motivated others to give, especially because everyone loved Stevie Ray Vaughan's music so much and knew what a legend he was. I was very touched by the heart of his mother as she was moved by God to get involved.

Another couple that stepped up to help at that time was Pastor Sam and Becky Carr, my pastors from Word of Life Center in Shreveport, Louisiana. Pastor Carr was a big fan of Stevie Ray Vaughan, and he and his wife, Becky, decided to match that amount. After that, God continued to bless and bless, and He also continued to open the doors for us to share the vision of what we were doing.

November 15, 1995 was a proud moment as Martha Sundquist, the wife of the then Governor of Tennessee, along with myself and music artists Naomi Judd and Point of Grace hosted a ribbon-cutting ceremony to signify that the home was completed debt-free and ready to open. Over 500 people crammed into the doors of Mercy Ministries that Wednesday afternoon. We were amazed at the level of excitement and anticipation!!

In just a few months time, the home was fully staffed and completely filled with girls. It became apparent to us after a couple of years of operating the home that it was now time for us to build our national ministry headquarters in Nashville. Once again, we went to the architect and had architectural plans and an artist rendering drawn. We gathered cost estimates and began to speak out the vision to the people. It was at that time that a very generous donor came forward and gave a significant amount of money to begin a matching funds challenge that actually ended up paying for the entire building by the time it was all matched!

We moved into this three-story, 15,000 square foot building, once again debt-free, in 2002. When we first moved into the building, it seemed so big and we wondered if we would ever fill it up. Today, we have three floors of office space completely filled, and we are making plans to add on because we don't have enough space to house all of the growth that

God has brought about. Let me explain some of the things that have happened so you will understand why we have out-grown this space.

It wasn't long after we moved into our office building that Dave and Joyce Meyer, two of our biggest supporters for Mercy Ministries, contacted us about building a home in St. Louis. God had put in Dave and Joyce's heart for Joyce Meyer Ministries to fund a Mercy home in the St. Louis area. Their ministry bought 32 acres of property for $1.8 million dollars. The property had previously been a Christian camp-ground and had a large Christian retreat center on it, but it was badly in need of renovations. As it turned out, Joyce Meyer Ministries not only paid for the land and deeded it over to Mercy Ministries, but they also provided the additional $1 million it took to pay for the renovations of the building!!

We continue to marvel at God's provision. The best way I know how to explain how God has provided is that when God's people get involved with what is close to His heart, which is healing broken hearts and restoring broken lives, then God gets involved in making a way when there seems to be no way.

September 28, 2005 was a very special day as Dave and Joyce Meyer gathered with Nick and Christine Caine from Sydney, Australia, and Contemporary Christian Artists, BarlowGirl, along with Mercy friends and supporters to offi-cially cut the ribbon. Together we dedicated this home to be used as a place of healing and restoration for countless num-bers of girls in the months and years to come. What a time of celebration it was!! With the opening of the St. Louis home, there were 30 additional beds for us to fill with girls who had been on our waiting list for so long.

It was around the time that the St. Louis home was being renovated that we were contacted by Buzz Oates, a prominent commercial real estate developer from Sacramento, California. Buzz Oates is a very generous man with strong

Christian faith, and God put it in his heart to finance the building of a new home in the Sacramento area. He visited the Nashville home, many meetings transpired, and out of that he donated a piece of property worth $1.5 million and gave us an additional $2.5 million toward our next home in Lincoln, California. That home is being built even as I write this and will be ready to take in 40 more girls by the end of 2008.

While the Sacramento home has been in process, the doors have opened for other homes in the United States. God directed us to some property in Santa Rosa, Florida, between Destin and Panama City in August of 2007. We purchased 12 acres of prime property at a very low price for the purpose of establishing another Mercy Ministries home.

In addition, while we were closing on the Florida property, I was invited by Pastors Derek and Sarah Turner to Charlotte, North Carolina to speak at their church, The Branch Family Church. When I arrived, the Turners took me out and showed approximately 50 acres of land where they plan to build their new church home. I rejoiced with them about how beautiful the property was because I just love to see other people's visions coming to pass. Then they took me to another piece of property across the road, which was about eight acres. They proceeded to tell me that they also own that property, and that God had put it in their hearts to give that property to Mercy Ministries for the purpose of building a home in the Charlotte area. This is another opportunity in front of us that we are pursuing.

In addition, a gentleman from Michigan contacted us about giving us a piece of property there, and we are in the process of working that out as well. So, we currently have three pieces of property that need homes built on them. Even as we have the Sacramento home going up, our three homes are always filled with girls.

It seems like the more girls we help, the more girls that call us for help. Even though we now have 90 available beds in the U.S. with our 20-bed home in Louisiana, our 40-bed home in Nashville, and our 30-bed home in St. Louis, our waiting list has only continued to grow. At any one given period of time, we have about 700 girls on our waiting list. We continue praying and believing to be able to open more homes in the U.S. because the need is so great.

Not only are we dealing with drug addictions, pregnancy, and sexual abuse, but, at this time, there is a great number of eating disorders and cutting that is taking place among the youth of our nation. These two issues have reached epidemic proportions. At Mercy Ministries, we are seeing many young women set free from these addictions – young women that have been told by the experts of the world that they are hopeless and incurable. We know that Christ is the answer; thus, our prayer that more homes will be built so that we can freely share the message of Christ.

Now, let me bring you fully up to date. About three weeks before Christmas in 2007 (just a few weeks ago from the time of this writing), I received a call from Joel Osteen, pastor of Lakewood Church in Houston, Texas. I have a close relationship with the entire Osteen family, and I highly value my friendship with them. They have supported Mercy over the years, and Joel's sister and brother-in-law, Lisa and Kevin Comes, have adopted their three children through our adoption agency, including a set of twins who are now almost 10 years old and a son who is now almost 7 years old. Every time Joel speaks of his nieces and nephew, he cries because they are so close to his heart.

Just a few weeks ago, I received a call from Joel. He began to tell me that he felt that it was time for him and his wife Victoria to get involved with Mercy Ministries in a big way. After praying, they believe they are to give a large amount of money personally, and for Lakewood to match that amount to bring Mercy Ministries to Houston. We plan to have a press conference later this year to announce this pro-

posed new home. We have already begun the process of looking at properties, and we are believing for the right location.

If you are reading this, please say a prayer for us because
there is a mission field right here in America, and we want to
do our best to fulfill our God-given assignment. Perhaps God
is speaking to you to become a monthly partner with us if you
have not already done so. Your partnership will mean an
investment in seeing captives set free and in raising up the
next generation of God-given leaders! Since books become
outdated the moment they are written, I highly urge you to
visit our website at www.mercyminsitries.com to get an
update of all that is happening with the ministry currently.

International Homes Established

Mark and Darlene Zschech from Sydney, Australia first
walked through the doors of Mercy Ministries in 1999 while
we were in the process of building our office building.
Darlene Zschech has become known around the world as the
worship leader for Hillsong Church in Sydney. She also
authored the song "Shout to the Lord" that is also well-known
all over the world.

In the year 1995, I felt prompted to begin praying about
Australia. I wasn't sure why, but somehow I realized the
urgency and began to pray. I had never been to Australia, and
I knew no one who lived there. It didn't make sense, but I
began to pray anyway.

About the same time I began praying about Australia, a
friend of Darlene's in California mailed her a copy of the first
edition of the same book you are now reading, *Echoes of
Mercy*. After reading this book, Darlene knew in her heart
that she was somehow to be connected with Mercy
Ministries. Darlene's husband, Mark, connected with the
vision as well. They both recognized the work of Mercy
Ministries of America to be the same dream that God had put
in their hearts years earlier for their own country.

The same Holy Spirit that was prompting me to pray about Australia was also prompting Mark and Darlene to pray about a ministry like Mercy Ministries to come to their nation. Being mature believers, Mark and Darlene understood the instruction of God's Word in Habakkuk 2:3 which says, "For the vision is yet for an appointed time and it hastens to the end (fulfillment); it will not deceive or disappoint. Though it tarry, wait (earnestly) for it, because it will surely come; it will not be behind hand on its appointed day" (Amplified Bible).

Knowing the vision was for an appointed time, Mark and Darlene committed their dream to prayer, fully knowing that God would bring it forth in His time. Four years later, God caused our paths to cross, which both Darlene and Mark had fully expected God to do at some point. When we met on April 16, 1999, we knew it was a day of destiny. This was Mark and Darlene's first trip to Nashville, and they asked the president of their record company if he would arrange for them to have a tour of Mercy and to meet me if I was in town.

That day of destiny produced a supernatural hookup, a divine connection brought about by God Himself! So much has happened in such a short time! Why? Because it was God's appointed time. When God is ready to birth a vision that has been conceived in the Spirit, and prayed into existence through intercession, no demon in hell can stop it!

The official launching of Mercy Ministries Australia took place at the "Colour Your World 2000" National Women's Conference in Sydney, Australia March 16-22. Approximately 4,000 women were in attendance, including 86 international delegates. The conference was hosted by Senior Pastors Brian and Bobbie Houston of Hillsong Church, who gave their blessing and created the platform for Mercy Ministries Australia to be made known throughout the nation. The response was overwhelming and unprecedented, as hearts were moved to get involved.

During this women's conference, I had the awesome privilege of sharing the platform with Darlene Zschech to speak forth the vision of Mercy Ministries Australia. Joining with us to share her incredible story of healing and restoration was Jenni Fairbairn, the first international graduate of Mercy Ministries of America, who is a native of Sydney, Australia. Jenni worked tirelessly throughout the conference working the information table and talking to hundreds of people one on one. Jenni became a full-time staff member, working under the direct leadership of Mark and Darlene Zschech for a season of time. She traveled all over the nation with Darlene and others sharing the vision of Mercy Ministries Australia. The rest is history.

Property was purchased in Sydney, Australia to open the first home, and now we have a second home open on the Sunshine Coast in Queensland. A third home is being built in Adelaide and is scheduled to open in just a few weeks. We have also purchased property in Perth, and we are planning for future expansion in the nation of Australia.

This all happened because of the divine connection that God set up for His purposes. As a result of this divine connection with Mark and Darlene Zschech, which began in April of 1999, I have made over 30 trips to Australia to speak in various conferences including Hillsong and Colour Your World conferences established by Brian and Bobbie Houston, pastors of Hillsong Church. Through these conferences, I have met many other pastors and Christian leaders from many nations around the world.

As a result of those relationships that have been established, we also opened a home in the United Kingdom, near Bradford, England, which came about because of the divine connection with Paul and Glenda Scanlon of Abundant Life Church.

There is also a home now open in Auckland, New Zealand that came forth as a result of a divine connection with Pastors Paul and Maree de Jong of LIFE Church in Auckland.

It was also through the Color Your World Conference that I met pastors John and Helen Burns, who have also partnered with us to bring Mercy Ministries to Canada. The first home is planned for the Vancouver area.

Another divine connection that occurred through our Australian connection was Robert and Karyn Barriger from Lima, Peru. Their daughter was dying from an eating disorder and was told by the experts that she would not live. She chose to come into the Sydney, Australia home and was one of the first girls who graduated from that program. Her life was so dramatically transformed that everyone who knew her was astounded. Today she is in full-time ministry with her husband and has given birth to her first child. I had the privilege of going to Lima, Peru a couple of years ago to launch the vision of Mercy Ministries, and this young woman served as my interpreter. What a joy it was as we both shed tears while she interpreted her own story as I told it. The people in her country were so moved, and we are in the process of opening the first Peru home in the Lima area.

Last, but not least, we have also established a strong relationship with Pastors Andre and Wilma Olivier in Johannesburg, South Africa. I have been there several times to speak the vision of Mercy Ministries so we can expand to that nation as well, and we now feel that it is time to move forward. So, it's only a matter of time until the first home opens in that nation.

As you can tell, God is on the move! His heart is for the hurting, desperate people who are crying out for freedom. You can be a part of making freedom possible. You can be a highway of freedom that others can walk on through your support and partnership. Thank you for literally making the difference between life and death. Please keep us in your prayers as we move forward to help establish God's Kingdom on this earth as our Lord and Savior Jesus Christ prayed in Matthew 6:9-13, commonly known as the Lord's Prayer. "Your Kingdom come, Your will be done on Earth as it is in Heaven."

Conclusion

Where Do We Go from Here?

> *But be doers of the word, and not hearers only, deceiving yourselves. For if anyone is a hearer of the word and not a doer, he is like a man observing his natural face in a mirror; for he observes himself, goes away, and immediately forgets what kind of man he was. But he who looks into the perfect law of liberty and continues in it, and is not a forgetful hearer but a doer of the work, this one will be blessed in what he does. (James 1:22-25)*

Now what?

Where do we go from here?

To begin with, if you know of any troubled girl or unwed mother who needs a time of intensive discipleship and a place to stay, please don't hesitate to contact Mercy Ministries. We would like to help her.

The time is *now*. Perhaps God is calling you to make a contribution to Mercy Ministries. If the Holy Spirit is speaking to your heart, I pray that you will take advantage of His invitation and take part in this work of restoration. We must fight abortion with God's vision, not with man's.

Please pray that our ministry to troubled girls and unwed mothers will continue to bring restoration to broken lives, and also that the Holy Spirit will spread our vision of extending mercy throughout His church. Without the help of the church,

Mercy Ministries would be powerless to give hurting women the substantial spiritual healing they so desperately need.

Finally, I hope you will be inspired by what you have read and will become obedient to the Lord's command to heal the brokenhearted, proclaim deliverance to the captives, and set at liberty those who are bound. Take time to pray and search for God's guidance as to how you can actively demonstate His mercy to those who need it. God has called every Christian to minister to the needs of others wherever He has placed them.

If your heart has been stirred by what you have read, there are two specific ways you can help us.

We need faithful supporters who wish to become "Treasure Builders" with Mercy Ministries by giving monthly. "Treasure Builder" members enable us not only to continue what we are presently doing but to expand this ministry.

While we greatly appreciate large contributions, it is the faithful people who give what they can month after month that enable us to continue this good work. It is because of this ongoing support that Mercy Ministries is making an impact.

If you want to give a major gift to help in establishing another home, we welcome your support. If you want to become actively involved, please see the following page for additional information.

Together we can make a difference!

Check out our **website** at <u>www.mercvministries.com</u> to find out more information about Mercy Ministries and information regarding the following:

- How to become a financial donor
- To obtain an application for admission
- For national and international locations of Mercy Ministries' homes
- To receive information about our adoption services
- To receive the quarterly newsletter
- To purchase product resources

Mercy Ministries of America asks that you please contact our National Headquarters in Nashville, Tennessee for additional information regarding the following:

- Speaking Engagements
- Employment Opportunities
- Volunteer Opportunities
- All Other Inquiries

Mercy Ministries of America
P.O. Box 111060
Nashville, TN 37222-1060
Phone: (615) 831-6987
Fax: (615) 315-9749
Email: info@mercyministries.com
Website: www.mercyministries.com